matthew
apostle and evangelist

matthew
apostle and evangelist

by EDGAR J. GOODSPEED

THE JOHN C. WINSTON COMPANY

PHILADELPHIA · TORONTO

The Library of Congress has cataloged this book as follows:

Goodspeed, Edgar Johnson, 1871–
    Matthew, apostle and evangelist. [1st ed.] Philadelphia, Winston [1959]

    159 p. 21 cm.

25731

    1. Matthew, Saint, apostle. 2. Bible. N. T. Matthew—Criticism, interpretation, etc.

BS2495.G6   225.92   59–6599 ‡

Library of Congress

Made in the United States of America

In Abiding Memory of
Elfleda
1880–1949

contents

isaiah in matthew

ISAIAH 7:14
"The maiden will be pregnant and will have a son,
And they will name him Immanuel" Matt. 1:23.

ISAIAH 40:3
"Hark! Someone is shouting in the desert,
'Get the Lord's way ready!
Make his paths straight!'" Matt. 3:3.

ISAIAH 9:1f
"Zebulon's land, and Naphtali's land,
Along the road to the sea, across the Jordan,
Galilee of the heathen!
The people that were living in darkness
Have seen a great light,
And on those who were living in the land of the shadow of
    death
A light has dawned!" Matt. 4:15–16.

ISAIAH 53:4
"He took our sickness and carried away our diseases." Matt.
8:17.

ISAIAH 61:1
"The blind are regaining their sight . . .
and good news is being preached to the poor." Matt. 11:5.

ISAIAH 14:13–15
"Are you to be exalted to the skies?
You will go down among the dead!" Matt. 11:23.

ISAIAH 42:1–4, see also Isa. 41:8, 9
"Here is my servant whom I have selected,
My beloved, who delights my heart!
I will endow him with my Spirit,
And he will announce a judgment to the heathen.
He will not wrangle or make an outcry,
And no one will hear his voice in the streets;
He will not break off a bent reed,
And he will not put out a smoldering wick,
Until he carries his judgment to success.
The heathen will rest their hopes on his name!"
                                        Matt. 12:18–21.

Isaiah 6:9, 10
" 'You will listen and listen, and never understand,
And you will look and look, and never see!
For this nation's mind has grown dull,
And they hear faintly with their ears,
And they have shut their eyes,
So as never to see with their eyes,
And hear with their ears,
And understand with their minds, and turn back,
And let me cure them!' Matt. 13:14, 15.

Isaiah 29:13
" 'This people honor me with their lips,
Yet their hearts are far away from me.
But their worship of me is all in vain,
For the lessons they teach are but human precepts.' " Matt.
15:8, 9.

Isaiah 62:11
"Tell the daughter of Zion,
'Here is your king coming to you,
Gentle, and riding on an ass,
And on the foal of a beast of burden.' " Matt. 21:5.

Isaiah 56:7
'My house shall be called a house of prayer,' Matt. 21:13.

Isaiah 5:1f
"There was a land owner who planted a vineyard and
fenced it in, and hewed out a wine-vat in it, and built a
watch-tower, . . ." Matt. 21:33.

Isaiah 19:2
"For nation will rise in arms against nation,
And kingdom against kingdom," Matt. 24:7.

Isaiah 13:10; cf. 34:4
"the sun will be darkened,
and the moon will not shed its light,
and the stars will fall from the sky,
and the forces of the sky will shake." Matt. 24:29.

Isaiah 27:13
"with a loud trumpet-call," Matt. 24:31
—an allusion to Isaiah 27:13—
On that day will a blast be blown on a great trumpet;

1

matthew,
apostle and evangelist

OUR generation has witnessed a notably increased appreciation of Matthew as the greatest of the first-century gospels, along with a very general abandonment of its authenticity as the work of the apostle whose name it bears. In fact, it is very hard for us to think of anybody really equal to writing the Gospel of Matthew. We are faced with this paradox: As Matthew has gone up in favor and esteem, it has declined in authenticity as an apostolic writing. We have, in effect, been driven by its very excellence to feel that it is too good for any one of those twelve Galilean disciples to have written.

This is in part due to the more realistic modern approach to the apostles. As we view them in the gospels, they impress us as a very ordinary group of Galilean working people, though not quite peasants; for Simon and Andrew and the sons of Zebedee, with their boats and employees, must have made up quite a concern. They sold their fish to the drying plants at Tarichea, across the lake, which took its name from that industry. (*Tarichos* means a smoked fish.) But except in their splendid readiness to leave all and follow Jesus, they strike us as very ordinary men, quite unlikely to burst forth with a new type of religious literature so overwhelmingly successful as the written gospel.

Along with this has gone a feeling that the apostles did not really amount to very much after all. The great Christian mission which so soon swept over the Roman world and the adjacent eastern lands like Parthia and Armenia, we vaguely feel, did not owe too much to their activities. None of them, certainly, found such a historian as Paul did. And yet, as M. S. Enslin has lately reminded us, the work went on widely and effectively, if obscurely, spread by the apostles who went out into the world.

The silence of the Book of Acts about their specific labors is no doubt mainly due to the fact that they had gone forth from Galilee in different directions in obedience to Jesus' recorded order to go into all the world and preach the gospel, perhaps twenty years before Luke himself came on the scene, in A.D. 49–50.

We find ourselves, to our surprise, by no means strangers to Matthew's family, the household of Alpheus; James, the son of Alpheus, was one of the apostles, and his mother was a witness of the Crucifixion. Apart from Matthew's abrupt call and his response to it, he appears in the first three Gospels only in the lists of the apostles, which with that in Acts 1:13 contain only the barest mention of his name. Let us look more closely at the Gospel of

Matthew, to see what further light it may have to throw upon the identity of its writer. We shall find the writer curiously adept in figures, and not unwilling to record stories or "parables" involving huge sums of money, like the slaves and the talents they were commissioned to invest; a talent was worth about a thousand dollars, and one slave was trusted with five talents, and succeeded in making five more!

But it is in the story of the Unforgiving Debtor that Matthew deals with his largest figures. The debtor's obligation, ten thousand talents, may be variously computed, perhaps at ten million dollars. It is this that his royal creditor so generously forgives. Yet this debtor turns on one of his own poor debtors and throws him into prison for a mere hundred denarii—in purchasing power worth about a hundred dollars. Here we are pretty clearly in the tax collector's vocabulary. This is high finance in the writer's world, at least in imagination. Indeed, the introduction of the story, Peter's question as to how many times he must forgive his brother who wrongs him, fairly baffles the modern translator or interpreter. Does it mean seventy-seven times, or seventy times seven times? Probably the former, making old Lamech's ratio of revenge in Genesis 4:24 the believer's ratio of forgiveness.

The modern reader asks himself, What could have moved an ex-tax collector like Matthew to write this extraordinary account of Jesus' ministry and make it so amazingly rich in Jesus' teaching? This is a fair question, surely. But we must not confuse it with a denial that he did so. We must first inquire with candor into the elements in the situation that might have stimulated such action on Matthew's part, and his probable capacities for responding to it. Too little serious attention, we may find, has been devoted to these two matters, though they are obviously of the greatest importance to the solution of the problem of the Gospel of Matthew.

2

who was matthew?

THE Greek word for apostle occurs once in Matthew, once in John, twice in Mark, six times in the Gospel of Luke, and twenty-eight times in the Acts. So far is Matthew from stressing that office! Only in 10:2 does Matthew call the Twelve "apostles."

The apostles are spoken of as the Twelve, or the twelve disciples, eight times in Matthew against ten times in Mark and six times in Luke.

The name Matthew—in Greek, Matthaeus—does not occur in the Old Testament or the Apocrypha, nor is it found in Greek papyri of New Testament times. Noeldeke seventy-five years ago suggested that it might be a late form of Amittai, the father of Jonah, Jonah 1:1, II Kings 14:25, formed by the dropping of the unaccented first syllable, and in this he has been followed by a number of distinguished scholars—Ewald, Hitzig, Schmiedel.

Matthew is clearly identical with Levi the son of Alpheus, of Mark 2:14 and Luke 5:27–29; for the call and the dinner that followed it clearly have reference to the same disciple, who in Matthew's account of the same incident, 9:9–13, is called Matthew. Alpheus is often mentioned in connection with various disciples. James, the ninth apostle in Mark's list, 3:18, is called the son of Alpheus, as in Matthew 10:3, Luke 6:15, Acts 1:13. Matthew speaks of James' mother as Mary, 27:56, as does Mark also, 15:40 and 16:1, and Luke, in Luke 24:10. This James then must have been Matthew's brother, or half brother. Mark also speaks of a Joses, 15:40, 47, a follower of Jesus, as a son of Alpheus.

Alpheus' wife Mary was one of the heroic women who witnessed the Crucifixion, Mark 15:40; they even stayed on through those six terrible hours and witnessed Jesus' death. After that, they waited until his body was taken down from the cross and carried away to burial. They actually saw where he was buried. They returned to his burial place the morning after the Sabbath, saw the risen Jesus, and took his message for the Twelve.

This extraordinary woman is spoken of as the mother of James and Joses, but not as the mother of Matthew; we must suppose she was his step-mother. While all this tells us little about Alpheus, it outlines a family of extraordinary loyalty and significance in the Christian group. It is natural to suppose that Matthew was a member of this family, and as things turned out, the most important male member of it. It may even suggest the background of his very dramatic call. Were not James and Joses half brothers of Matthew and sons of Alpheus and Mary? Were not James and Matthew apostles, and Matthew the greatest of the evangelists? If so, we seem to be in the presence of the most remarkable household in the primitive church; devoted, gifted, heroic! Little is said indeed of Alpheus and his attitude in all this, perhaps because with such a family he was too well known to call for a personal eulogy; for the fact that he is referred to as the head of the family, the father of these sons, and the husband of this Mary, tells its own story. Clearly, he is used to identify the members of his family, as though he were himself well known.

The question to be faced by those who deny authorship by Matthew is, Why should the book be ascribed to him? He is given prominence in Mark because of his official and financial position as a tax collector, it would seem, though under the name of Levi (2:14)—Levi, the son of Alpheus, sitting at the tollhouse. But Levi does not appear among the Twelve; there, the seventh apostle is Matthew, Mark 3:18. Luke, too, prefers the name Matthew, 6:14; Acts 1:13. Perhaps the name Levi was too deeply saturated with Judaism (for the evangelists) to be admitted to the list of apostles. It was the name of the priestly tribe, and the tribe most deeply connected with Jewish religious groups, priests and Levites, and the whole cult of the temple. But if so, whence came the name Matthew? It would not have been a recommendation of Matthew for the unmerited honor of being the chief evangelist that he was, so to speak, a reformed tax collector, nor that as Levi he was, tribally speaking, the most deep-rooted Jew of them all!

By descent and by profession Matthew seems a

most unpromising candidate for the high place of
chief of the gospel writers—unless his semipriestly
background and his professional techniques
uniquely equipped him for that actual duty! That
is to say, if he did not write the greatest Gospel,
was he not the last man who would have been
thought of in connection with it? He was of a tribe
for centuries identified with formal Judaism and by
personal profession virtually a renegade from it!
What but the sheer logic of facts could have prevailed over these two well-nigh insurmountable ob-
stacles: his ancestral Judaism, of the deepest dye,
and his personal identification with a despised and
hated calling? And yet, paradoxically, he emerges
upon the pages of history as Jesus' greatest interpreter. It is a fair question whether these difficulties
have ever been fairly met. For the most part they
seem to have been quietly evaded.

The abrupt call of Matthew, in Mark 2:14, is at
first obscure and perplexing to the reader; it is the
only individual call of an apostle in the Synoptic
Gospels. Yet to the evangelist, the congruity must
have been apparent and even obvious. The pardon
of the paralytic, in the synagogue: "Your sins are
forgiven;" brings from the scribes a charge of
blasphemy, ("Who can forgive sins but God
alone?"), a most serious accusation on their part,
in view of the express command of Leviticus 23:16:

"Whoever blasphemes the name of the Lord must
be put to death by having the whole community
stone him!"

This fearful peril, so narrowly escaped, must have

awakened Jesus to the shattering thought that his
life might be snuffed out at any wayside synagogue
where the scribes' charge might be caught up
against him. It would need no government action,
no trial and conviction; if the scribes could con-
vince the congregation, the congregation could act
at once and put him to death then and there. In
fact, and in short, his life was no longer safe.

But Jesus had no mind to give up his life without
having uttered his message which he so highly valued. It must not perish with him! That should not
happen.

Must not the thought of Isaiah have come back to
him now with surpassing force? Isaiah, too, had had
a great message, but he had confided it to a group
of disciples, who preserved and afterward published it. Isaiah died a martyr's death, being sawn
asunder by the cruel king Manasseh. But that was
only after Isaiah's long and fruitful ministry of some
forty years. When he was threatened and felt his
foes closing in upon him, Isaiah had said,

"I will bind up my testimony, and seal my teaching in the heart of my disciples. Then I will wait
for the Lord, who is hiding his face from the house
of Israel; I will set my hope on him." 8:16–18.

No prophet stood higher in the mind of Jesus
than Isaiah. His quotations from him as they appear in Matthew are numerous and extended;
printed as poetry, they now fill more than a page.
This verse from Isaiah is not among them, but it
seems unmistakably to have been in Jesus' mind as
he strides away from the seething synagogue and

along the seashore. Presently, the tax office, with Matthew, the son of Mary and Alpheus, sitting in it at work over his books, catches his eye. The tax collector is the very man; the village or town clerk, keeping the taxbooks from day to day, as the Greek papyri have so pathetically shown us. He is the man for books and records, and of such a man Jesus has suddenly come to feel the need. Why, Isaiah had such men, and he must have them, too. Someday the scribes may triumph and succeed in stopping his mouth! Without a moment's hesitation, it would seem, Jesus catches the eye of Matthew and calls to him,

"Follow me!"

And Matthew gets right up and follows him!

Was he wrong about Matthew? Many people think so. They can make nothing of this passage, and relegate the incident to the inexplicable class. But with Isaiah as our guide, we find in it the key to Jesus' precautions. He now has a secretary, a recorder, such as Isaiah and Jeremiah had, to such tremendous advantage! Mark does not explain the reason and result of this impulsive action, because he assumes that the close and attentive reader will see the point himself. Moreover, Matthew was still alive and at work. Peter had told him the story at Rome, and Mark thinks it worth writing into his memoirs of Peter.

As for Matthew, is it not a fact that we know him better than any other of the twelve apostles, except perhaps Peter? He was a tax collector, at Capernaum, the son of Alpheus; his mother, or stepmother, was that extraordinary woman Mary, who actually witnessed the Crucifixion, agony, and death of Jesus! She saw him taken down from the cross and followed his body to the place of its burial, which she witnessed. What incredible devotion! She was one of the three women who came on the Sunday morning to anoint Jesus' body, found the tomb empty and beheld the angel and Jesus himself, as Matthew so strikingly records, 28:5–10.

Matthew was the brother, or half brother, it would seem, of the apostle James the Less and of Joses, or Joseph, so that with such a stepmother and two such brothers, he is tied into the gospel story as no one else is; consider the family of Alpheus, from Matthew's call, to his stepmother's being charged with Jesus' last message to the disciples,

"Tell my brothers to go to Galilee, and they will see me there!"

Here was a man brought into the gospel narrative by his stepmother, his brothers, and his own call and experience as was no other follower of Jesus, not even Peter himself! No, we are in no uncertainty or ignorance about Matthew the tax collector of Capernaum, and the family to which he belonged.

And did he then fade away into silence? Or did he rather consummate and crown all this by writing the greatest of the Gospels? Well, why not? Who was better prepared? Particularly if Jesus, following Isaiah's great precedent, had encouraged him to do so? Jesus' call of Matthew, so featured in the earliest Gospels, certainly invites that conclusion. And the

appearance of Matthew's Gospel within ten years,
presumably, of Mark's, would have demanded some
distinctive name for the new Gospel, in an age so
insistent upon specific authorship and in a city like
Antioch, the missionary headquarters of the world-
wide church. What were they to call it?

It is a mistake to look for an ordinary man as the
author of the Gospel according to Matthew. Whoever he was, he was not an ordinary man. It was
no ordinary man who wrote a Gospel which Renan,
the French critic, eighteen hundred years later,
could call the most important book in the world.
How many of our current best sellers will still be
leading human thought in A.D. 3600?

Of course, living for even six months in the company of Jesus, hearing him talk and asking him
questions, would be an education of the most intensive kind. And if a man could write and was accustomed to writing, he could hardly help putting
some things down. A tax collector was used to doing
just that. It was his lifelong habit. In Mark's account, it is just after Herod's agents and the Pharisees plot to kill Jesus that he chooses the Twelve as
his special apostles, 3:14. Matthew follows his account of this purpose of the Pharisees with a long
quotation—ten lines of poetry—from Isaiah, 12:17–
21, which he applies to Jesus, as God's beloved
servant. He is not insensible of Jesus' deep interest
in Isaiah and his work and fate, doubtless including
that tragic valedictory, Isaiah 8:16–18.

Certainly, it was precisely the fact that he had
bound up his testimony and sealed his teaching in

the hearts of his disciples that had carried Isaiah's message on to influence and power for seven hundred years, unhindered by his untimely martyrdom. It is interesting to see that of Matthew's quotations from the Old Testament, as Dr. F. J. A. Hort reckons them, between one-fifth and one-sixth (twenty-one out of a hundred and twenty-three) are from Isaiah. The only Old Testament book that at all rivals Isaiah in number of reflections in Matthew is the Psalms, the echoes and quotations of which are reckoned at twenty-one as are those of Isaiah, in Westcott and Hort's *New Testament in Greek*, pp. 531, 532. This is due to the number of echoes of Psalm 22, in the twenty-seventh chapter of Matthew, with its terrific account of the Crucifixion. (That account might well be terrific, if Matthew's stepmother had witnessed it! Could she ever forget it?) The language of the psalm colors the agonizing narrative no less than seven times in this chapter. But in the amount of text quoted in the Gospel of Matthew, Isaiah far surpasses the Psalter; and of course the Psalter is not the work of one author, it is a whole hymnbook. No other Old Testament author or book so influenced Matthew as Isaiah did. We have seen that Matthew's quotations from Isaiah, if printed as poetry would occupy more than a page.

These facts are assembled here for their bearing upon the influence of Isaiah, not only as a book but as a person, a martyr to his prophetic vocation and yet in the long perspective of history how victorious over his ruthless foes! This influence is peculiarly striking, in the pages of the man who beyond all others did a similar work for Jesus and his message— a far greater work than had been done for Isaiah by his disciples.

In the three fourteens of the genealogy it is the man of figures—the tax collector!—who speaks. To him figures are eloquent. It is not so much the identities of Jesus' ancestors that matter, it is the fact that the line, exalted as it was, reached its climax in him, as the one who began the seventh seven. This is hardly less than the sign manual of the tax-collector apostle, who thus authenticates his book for those who have eyes to see! If so, it is discouraging to observe how few of Matthew's modern interpreters have detected his device.

While Matthew, for I feel that it must have been he, has taken some liberties with the list materials in Kings to obtain these results—he is really following I Chronicles 1–3 — such difficulties fall away if we remember that this title page is a work of the bookkeeper's art, rather than a dull ancestral chronicle.

To this experienced Christian teacher at Antioch, when the Jewish war of A.D. 66–70 was over and fast passing into history, comes the Gospel of Mark, written at Rome about A.D. 70, to preserve for the Roman believers what could still be remembered of Peter's eyewitness account of the work of Jesus. It names itself in its first line: "Here begins the good news [or gospel] of Jesus Christ." The first Christian book, it might well fall into the hands of this apostle, and with what intense interest he

would scan its columns. No one would be half so
stirred by it as such a man. It brings back old scenes
and journeys, in every one of which he had shared.
For these were the events of those brief months, as
Peter remembered them. Matthew finds it all of
exciting interest, and in it all he substantially agrees.
This was what had happened, at least as Peter saw
it. Some things are out of order, perhaps; with Peter
gone, Mark had no definite clue or guide to the sequence of the events. Yet the action is there, and
how vividly it all comes back to the old tax collector.

His second thought is of a fault. How weakly,
even blindly it begins! One hardly knows what is
the first sentence! It calls for an adequate introduction capable of interesting Jews and other religious
people in its unique and commanding message.

The oldest manuscripts that preserve the title of
the first Gospel—Sinaiticus, Vaticanus and the Beza
manuscript—all spell it with a double theta, "Math-
thaeus," th or theta being the eighth letter in the
Greek alphabet. The earliest manuscript yet discovered, the Chester Beatty gospels, about A.D.
200, while it begins with a closing fragment of
Matthew, does not show its name. It is mentioned,
however, in the fragment of Papias preserved in
Eusebius' *Church History*, 3:39.

Papias was a resident of Hierapolis in Phrygia
who made it his business to interview anyone who
passed that way from Palestine and inquire of them
for any memories of sayings of Jesus they might
have heard back in Syria, and these he faithfully re-

corded, about A.D. 140, in his book, called *Interpretations of the Sayings of the Lord.* Copies of this strange and intersting work existed in monastic libraries in the Tyrol and in the south of France until the thirteenth and fourteenth centuries, but have never been found since. Something about them can be learned from Irenaeus, in *Against Heresies,* 5:33: 3, 4, and Eusebius' *Church History,* 3:39, where Papias explains his interest in what the hearers of Jesus might have to tell about his sayings—Andrew, Peter, Philip, Thomas, James, John, Matthew, or any other disciples—"and what Aristion and the elder John say." Papias cared less for written books than for "the living and surviving voice." He records a very convincing statement about the origin of the Gospel of Mark and then says about Matthew, "So Matthew took down the sayings in the Aramaic language, and everyone interpreted them as well as he could."

As nothing is seriously known of such a work by Matthew as *The Sayings,* it is clear that Papias refers to such Aramaic notes as Matthew, tax collector that he was, took from day to day of Jesus' utterances, as he was evidently called to do, in the light of the action of Isaiah, when he saw the fate that threatened him, Isaiah 8:16–18. Obviously, Matthew was called by Jesus when he was threatened with death as Isaiah had been—a point too often overlooked. Tax collectors were not only proficient in writing but many of them knew shorthand, in Jesus' time and a hundred years before. While we cannot say that Matthew used it in taking down Jesus' utterances, it had been employed a hundred years before by the Roman senate when Cicero was consul, at his instance, in recording the speech of Cato the Younger in the Catiline debate. Even without it, dictation could be taken down with great speed; consider Paul's letters, sometimes, if not always, dictated to professional writers, to be taken down and written out later in fair copies, to be sent to his correspondents. By way of contrast, see Galatians 6:11. It is not at all necessary to understand Papias as meaning that Matthew published an Aramaic form of Jesus' sayings in a book or put it in circulation, though book publication was a well-known feature of Greek life in the first century. But up to the time of this writing, hardly one book originating in Aramaic has been reported. Matthew was doubtless the custodian as well as the writer of these notes, a duty for which his tax-collecting experience had well fitted him. All this, it will be observed, is in the realm not only of the possible but of the probable.

Except for Homer, the Greeks did not, like the Jews, exalt and canonize their oldest books. On the contrary, their interest in literature was not antiquarian, but modern and contemporary. These facts must be kept in mind as we examine the striking part the Greeks played in the development of Christian literature. If we jumble and blur Greek and Jewish attitudes in these literary inquiries, we shall find little but confusion. The Greek Christian public was not exploring Christian literature in search of the earliest discernible sources, but the latest and best formulation. And as we study the earliest Christian books, Greek of course, we must bear in mind the Greek concern for authorship; Who wrote this work? Not the earliest, crudest form of it, but the best and latest form; and, of course, who wrote it in Greek? What else mattered? They were readers of Greek and regarded other tongues, western or oriental, as virtually barbarous. This was the essence of the Greek literary genius. When a man wrote in Greek they recognized him as one of themselves—a civilized man! Modernity was their keynote. They must be up to date, and antiquity as such did not appeal to them. Luke fathomed it admirably in Acts 17:21: "For all Athenians and all visitors there from abroad used to spend all their time telling or listening to something new."

One consideration as to the authorship of Matthew is generally slighted, and yet it must be remembered and taken account of. It is the improbability in the Greek world of books and writers in which the Gospel of Matthew arose that its actual author should have been forgotten. For there are two major questions involved, if Matthew was not the true author. One is, how came the real author to have been set aside or forgotten? The other is, how did Matthew come to be nominated for the honor? Too little attention has been given to either of these questions, especially in the Greek world of authors and publishers. Yet it must be seen at once that each question is serious in the extreme.

Are we to suppose that the Gospel of Matthew

was an anonymous book, published without an author's name? Yet in the Greek world of books and authors in which the book certainly made its appearance, authorship was highly regarded and valued; anonymity had no place. Did the author then seek to disappear from sight, and offer his book anonymously? Or did he pseudonymously give it the name of Matthew, partly as a tribute to the apostle and partly to escape the responsibility of authorship? But could he have succeeded in this? And would he not probably have done as the publishers of John did, and added a supplement regarding its actual author, 21:24, 25? Yet the writer of Matthew deals with tremendous matters in a most powerful way (consider the first and the last of the six discourses), and seems hardly likely to have been capable of such feeble devices!

No, these two familiar considerations are more compatible with the genuineness of the traditional ascription than with any imaginable hypothesis of its fiction.

3

moδern attituδes
towarδ matthew

THE Gospel of Matthew is the most successful book ever written. It has had the largest circulation, exerted the greatest influence, and done the most good. Yet its authorship remains a problem. Who can possibly have written it?

It would not too much amaze us, would it, to find that Jesus himself had not a little to do with its inception, not to mention his contribution to its subject matter, for which he was largely responsible. Altogether it is a problem of the most startling, even amazing, possibilities.

Belief in the authorship of the Gospel of Matthew as by Matthew, the tax collector who became an apostle, was anciently held by Christian writers, but is now widely given up; as A. H. McNeile put it in 1914, and 1926, "the author was certainly not Matthew the apostle," *Commentary on Matthew,* p. xxviii.

I had long felt in this way myself. But the gradual crystallization of opinion upon Mark, Luke, and John of Ephesus as Gospel authors brings us back to the authorship of Matthew with a sounder point of view. What is the evidence for the apostle Matthew, in the present position of criticism? Does it not call for a faithful reconsideration? And what is there to be brought against it? Is Matthew the only one of the four not entitled to Gospel authorship?

The Greek writing propensities of the first-century tax collectors, revealed by the modern discoveries of the past half century or more, have enlarged and defined our conception of the literary possibilities of the tax-collector apostle Matthew. In fact, as we put together Jesus' pressing peril, his familiarity with the book of Isaiah—whose great message would have disappeared if it had not been for the capacities of his surviving disciples to record and thus perpetuate it—and Jesus' own early selection of a man able and accustomed to record matters in writing, we cannot escape the impression that this was something more than a happy accident. Later tradition certainly found in Matthew the tax-collector apostle the literary link with Jesus' utterances, and while this is scouted as absurd by much modern learning, it is certainly in order to review it. What likelier purpose in the face of Jesus' peril and Isaiah's example can Matthew's selection have had?

The writer of the Gospel of Matthew at once declares himself in his opening lines; he is a man of figures! He deals in them, he even toys with them! He carries Jesus' ancestry back to the founder of Judaism, Jacob (renamed Israel), and even to his grandfather Abraham. Following the line of Judah, in fourteen generations he brings us to David the King. Another cycle of fourteen kings of Israel or Judah brings us to the Exile, and fourteen more

brings us to Jesus. But why all these fourteens? The
writer offers no explanation; to him their significance
is obvious, and does not need to be spelled out for
the attentive reader. Here is a most amazing dis-
closure of the author's own qualifications and demands. He assumes that the reader will see at once
the significance of these lists! What manner of man
must he have been? He reveals—or conceals—himself on this first page. He is obviously a mathematician and a statistician, and so completely so that
he assumes his readers will be equally competent.
Alas, this has not always been the case!

As one explores the writings of modern scholars
on the Gospels, one must marvel at the skill with
which so many of them avoid the identity of the
writer of the Gospel of Matthew. The reader cannot escape some sense of disappointment that he
cannot find a definite judgment on the identity of
the author of the Gospel according to Matthew,
either pro or con, but most of the scholars are ret-
icent. It is perhaps enough for our survey purposes that they do not accept the apostle Matthew
in the capacity of author.

To return to the perplexing genealogy, G. H. Box
suggested, fifty years ago, that the three consonants
in David's name, d-v-d, were also figures in Hebrew,
4-6-4, making a total of fourteen!—which Box
thought made the genealogy "a sort of numerical
acrostic on the name David."

W. C. Allen, however, in his massive commentary on St. Matthew, (1907) p. 7, finds the
clue to the evangelist's motive in the mention

of the women—Tamar, Rahab, Ruth, Bathsheba; he thinks they are mentioned with an idea of defending Mary against Jewish slanders. This was also the view of Johannes Weiss. But C. J. G. Montefiore thought they were mentioned because they were known to the Old Testament story. They added color and interest to what was after all a very dull chronicle. Montefiore thought the genealogy had had a previous separate existence, and "was obviously only adopted and adapted by the evangelist." He also points out certain departures in it from the text of I Chronicles 1–3; Jeconiah "is counted as the first of the third series as well as the last of the second," p. 3, "there are errors in the second series: four kings are omitted—Ahaziah (son of Joram), Joash, Amaziah and Jehoiakim . . . In the first series, Rahab is oddly made the mother of Boaz . . . There must have been 300 years between them." (*Synoptic Gospels, II,* p. 4) Yet he could hardly expect the evangelist to be precise and say the "great, great, great grandmother" until eight or ten generations are accounted for, when he himself uses "father" in the sense of great, great, great . . . grandfather constantly; in fact, is there a commoner idiom? Take the children of Israel, for example; of course they are not, but his great, great, great . . . grandchildren, to the fortieth generation. And if this most familiar idiom can be thus loosely applied to grandfathers, why in the world not to grandmothers, too?

This is certainly one of the most hasty and inconsistent pieces of faultfinding (we cannot dignify it as criticism) ever flung at the long-suffering gene-alogy of Matthew. Indeed, the whole objection is negatived by the commonest of Hebrew idioms. The interpreter must make a fair effort at least to understand what the ancient writer is trying to say, before setting about to pick him to pieces! Monte-fiore's own work is not infallible; even in his "re-vised and corrected edition" (1927) he sometimes finds the spelling of James Moffatt's name perplex-ing. Of course, just as the Jews used "father" for forefather, or ancestor—"our father Abraham," Matthew 3:9, Luke 3:8, John 8:56—"mother" is used as ancestress—"Jerusalem . . . is our mother," Gala-tians 4:26. One might inquire how Montefiore would have improved this. With Matthew we are certainly in the hands of a writer of considerable imagination, and such criticisms as Montefiore offers reveal our literary limitations rather than Matthew's.

One must also mention Alfred Plummer's pains-taking commentary on Luke, (Scribner, 1910) in which he mentions "the fondness of our evangelist for numerical groups and especially for triplets. Hence the threefold division of the pedigree. The choice of fourteen may be explained as either twice seven, or as the numerical value of the three letters in the Hebrew name of David: 4 plus 6 plus 4 equals 14. In our present text the third division has only thirteen names, and elsewhere there is com-pression in order to get the right number. . . . The precise points of division are significant. In David (ver. 6) the family became royal; at the Captivity the royalty was lost (ver. 11); in 'Jesus who is called Christ,' (ver. 16) the royalty is recovered," p. 2. (*Christos* means anointed.) This will probably not weigh heavily with the American mind.

In none of these explanations, it seems to me, is the total structure of three fourteens adequately interpreted. It is simply the tax collector's way of saying, not flatly, but much more interestingly, "Jesus is the leading figure of the seventh seven, the climax of it all." It is precisely here that the tax collector's "figure-imagination" speaks so authoritatively: he thinks in numbers. Jesus is the climax of history; he begins its seventh seven! Beside this, these other explanations appear slight and inadequate. They have not caught the tax collector's mood and atmosphere. It is in this page that the author declares himself; he is the man of figures, the tax collector, the statistician.

The statement of Allen, in the *International Critical Commentary, St. Matthew,* p. lxxxi, that "there would be an irresistible tendency to find for it an apostolic sanction," shatters completely upon the fact that no such sanction was found for any other Gospel—Mark, Luke, or John the elder of Ephesus! Perhaps Allen had not observed the general disposition to call Greek books after the men who put them into Greek—Euclid, the Septuagint, Mark. On his theory of nomenclature, Mark should have been called Peter, under the irresistible tendency to find for it an apostolic sanction, a thing Mark shows no trace of! This irresponsible disposition to broad and alluring generalizations on Gospel authorship can be shown to be simply without foundation, in Greek Christian usage.

McNeile, in his volume, p. xxx, goes on to describe the "five orations" of Matthew's Gospel as "a second Torah corresponding with the five books of the Law," a most singular proceeding, when it is remembered that it was only when the Torah was translated into Greek that it was broken into five books, each with a Greek name—Genesis, Exodus, Leviticus, Numbers (Arithmoi), Deuteronomy—all Greek titles, given in the time of the Greek translation of the Torah. Manuscripts of the Hebrew Torah as far as I have seen them are not so broken, being continuous from what we know as Genesis 1:1 to Deuteronomy 34:12, though some Jewish halachists hold the fivefold division of the Torah to be of Massoretic origin, and trace it back to the time of the Second Temple! A Torah scroll sixty feet long is not unusual.

Moreover, the five orations credited to Matthew culminate, most unfortunately, in one which Jesus began to utter in the precincts of the Temple, within the walled city on the west bank of the Kedron, chapter 23, but was interrupted by his leaving the Temple and the city, crossing the Kedron and ascending the Mount of Olives, 24:1, 2. There he seats himself and in response to a question by the disciples, 24:3, addresses them, chapters 24, 25, but on another subject! The familiar five-sermon organization seems to neglect either chapter 23, the classic denunciation of the Pharisees, or chapters 24, 25, in which Jesus' moral teaching

reaches its climax in the Parable of the Judgment.
Worst of all, McNeile is oblivious of what is undoubtedly the most tremendous close ever uttered
by any orator in the world, 23:37–39, so deeply
moving, even heartbreaking:

O Jerusalem, Jerusalem! murdering the prophets, and
stoning those who are sent to her, how often I have
longed to gather your children around me, as a hen
gathers her brood under her wings, but you refused!
Now I leave you to yourselves. For I tell you, you will
never see me again until you say, "Blessed be he who
comes in the Lord's name!"

This moving farewell McNeile underestimates
completely, for he regards chapter 23 as just the
first part of the "fifth oration," embracing chapters
23, 24 and 25. And this although chapters 24 and
25 were on a very different subject, uttered elsewhere some hours later the same day, and to a
wholly different audience!

There are in fact six great discourses in Matthew,
and any analogy with the supposed so-called "five
books of Moses" (which were Greek, not Hebrew)
quite falls to the ground.

It was in his commentary that McNeile said of
the evangelist, "He was certainly not Matthew the
apostle," p. xxviii. His distinctive emphasis, McNeile
thinks, is upon Jesus as the Messiah of Jewish hope
and expectation, 16:16, though this with the preceding context, Matthew drew from Mark 8:29,
while adding Jesus' great response to Simon, ver.
17–19.

McNeile contends that "one who could write

with the paramount authority of an eyewitness would not have been content to base his work on that of a secondary authority." But in view of its relation to Peter, Mark can hardly be termed a "secondary authority"; and just such things do happen. I have seen writers who had been eyewitnesses of an educational drama, even active participants in it, seeking additional evidence of the larger picture from what might well be called "secondary authorities," whose memories and impressions they were not above consulting and even adopting, to give their work breadth and fulness. And if with modest and conscientious men in the twentieth century, why not in the first? Matthew's use of Mark, too, is far from uncritical; while he uses virtually all of it (except the poor woman casting her coin into the treasury) he transposes to such an extent that he may well be called the despair of the harmonist! Nor does Matthew precisely "base" his work upon Mark; he transposes Mark's sections mercilessly, using them where they fit his purpose. His view of Jesus is less the Man of Action, as Mark pictured him, than the Teacher, and for his great sermons he uses Mark's vivid narratives for frames! The fact that Matthew has so generally and so largely surpassed and transcended Mark and Luke shows that he knew what he was doing in using Mark, or sources later used by Luke in writing his book. That this does not suit our preconceived ideas of what such an evangelist should have done hardly matters. Let us remember, Matthew had never written a book before.

Canon F. W. Green, in his volume on St. Matthew in the Clarendon Press series, finds in Matthew a unique structure and pattern of its own. He holds that it has been carefully planned to consist of five books on five subjects:

The New Ethics of Jesus, and the Law, chapters 5–7

Concerning Apostleship, 9:36–11:1

The Hiding and Revelation of the Mystery, 13:1–53

The Problem of Church Unity, 18–19:1

The Messianic Judgment, 24–25

He is guided to this organization by the very similar formula with which each ends, "It came to pass that when Jesus had made an end of all these sayings."

Upon these discourses as they appear in Matthew, the influence of the Septuagint has been marked. Matthew's Greek, Green thinks, has been well described as "synagogue Greek," though the language of the synagogues of Palestine and even of Antioch was probably Aramaic. He had evidently not taken into account the possible influence of the tax collectors' Greek upon Matthew. Yet he quotes with approval C. F. Burney's remark that "Matthew more than any other evangelist has presented the sayings of Jesus as perhaps they were originally uttered, with all the rhythm and parallelism of Hebrew poetry," p. 7.

We are struck with the difficulty caused, in this fivefold analysis of the Matthean discourses, by the fact that there are so clearly six of them, as the evangelist reads, and while it is true that his occasional formula, "When Jesus had finished this discourse," or its equivalent, occurs after the Sermon on the Mount, 7:28, after the address to the Twelve. ("When Jesus had finished giving his twelve disciples these instructions," 11:1), after a dozen or more utterances in varied scenes and situations, 13:53, then after four chapters of varied movements and teachings, (14, 15, 16, 17—one-eighth of the Gospel) the discourse in chapter 18 is followed by the clause, "When Jesus had finished this discourse," 19:1.

The familiar formula, as an instrument for the analysis of the book, seems to be decidedly weakening. But when in order to make five discourses, we have to neglect the denunciation of the scribes and Pharisees in chapter 23 with what is without doubt the most powerful and moving conclusion in any of the discourses, or in any discourse ever uttered—the lament over Jerusalem and farewell to it, 23:37–39—to neglect this and build upon the jejune and formal "when Jesus had finished this discourse" seems more than a little absurd. Certainly there are six major discourses in Matthew, for that in chapter 23 is much more of a unit than is the miscellaneous mass of movements and encounters in chapters 13:54 to 17:27. Such an analysis would in fact probably be a surprise to the writer of Matthew. It is hardly reasonable to place the eighteenth chapter among the formal sermons of Jesus, interrupted as it is by Peter's coming up, and asking a question, suggested by next to the last thing Jesus

had said. Moreover, this particular fivefold sermon
organization disregards chapters 11:1 to 17:27,
amounting to one-fourth of the Gospel of Matthew,
uninterrupted by any recurrence of the expression
"when Jesus had finished this discourse," of which
so much is made, and culminating in the spirited
denunciation of the scribes and Pharisees, chapter
23, ending so dramatically in his reproach of Jerusalem and his unspeakably moving farewell to the
unrepentant city. Surely this chapter merits a place
among the great discourses! But the fivefold analysis of the Gospel of Matthew finds no place for it,
because it is not followed by the words "when Jesus
had finished this discourse."

The graver question is, of course, whether Jesus
and his Aramaic-speaking disciples thought of the
Torah of Moses as made up of the five books into
which their Greek translators had broken it, back in
the time of Philadelphus, some three hundred years
before. Certainly the Greek Christians of Antioch
probably used the Greek Septuagint as their form
of the Torah, and Matthew generally seems to em-
ploy it for his scripture quotations, yet he departs
widely from it for the Hebrew, in 12:18–22, perhaps
his longest Isaiah quotation; but his quotation of
Isaiah 6:9, 10, in 13:14, 15 follows the Septuagint
very closely, and is almost as long.

That the "Pentateuch," as the Greeks called it,
was in Hebrew one unbroken book, not five, is
interestingly shown by the amazing fact that the
second, third and fourth "books" of it begin, in
Hebrew, with the word "And."

There was of course no such division as McNeile assumes in the Torah, or Law of Moses. Synagogue manuscripts of the Torah to this day show nothing as far as I can learn of a fivefold division. That was strictly a Greek device, conditioned by Greek ideas of the convenient size for scrolls; to such ideas Hebrew scribes were entire strangers, even though all printed Hebrew Bibles adopt it! The Old Testament contains no allusion to five books on any subject. In fact, this plurality of Mosaic books is unknown to the Old Testament and also to the New; indeed, in Mark 12:26, Exodus 3:6 is quoted as from the Book of Moses, meaning the Torah. In Galatians 3:10, Deuteronomy 27:26 is quoted as speaking of "the Book of the Law" (Hebrew: "this Torah"). It is plain that the Jews regarded the whole of what we call by its Greek name the Pentateuch, as the Book of the Law. Synagogues today cherish the one long scroll containing what we have come to consider five separate books. They are not separated in the Hebrew scrolls.

They consequently form no Jewish precedent for a fivefold discourse in Matthew, nor does Matthew itself exhibit any such structure; the supposed fifth sermon is so evidently two addresses on different subjects and uttered in different scenes, one in the Temple, the other outside the city altogether, in some spot across the Kedron, upon the Mount of Olives. The fivefold structure simply has no Jewish existence in Moses, except as the Septuagint translators, whose tastes were strongly Greek, broke the

Torah into five convenient units, scroll-size. The Massoretic endorsement claimed for this is quite clearly a later adjustment.

Yet it is true that Matthew seems to reduce these six discourses of Jesus to five, throwing the fifth and sixth together by putting after the tremendous canvas of the Last Judgment his favorite refrain, "When Jesus had finished this discourse," 26:1 as in 7:28, 19:1, "When Jesus had finished giving his twelve disciples these instructions," 11:1, "When Jesus had finished these figures," 13:53. Yet chapter 23 with its "woes against the Pharisees" is as long as the discourse to the Twelve in chapter 10, and hardly less important. Moreover, Jesus leaves the temple, crosses the Kedron, and goes part way up the Mount of Olives before beginning, in response to their questions, the new discourse on the destruction of Jerusalem, 24:1–5. Any objective listing of his chief discourses would count them as six, the last one being in fact called forth by the disciples' questions, after his saying of the temple buildings,

"Do you see all this? I tell you, not one stone will be left here upon another but shall be torn down!"

As we survey the books of the New Testament, we are able to identify most of their authors with reasonable certainty—Mark; Luke (two volumes); John, his Gospel and three letters; Paul, with nine letters (or ten, if we include Ephesians); John the prophet of the Revelation—these five authors have contributed to the New Testament at least seventeen, or with Ephesians, eighteen of its twenty-seven books—in fact two-thirds of their numerical total, or in sheer bulk 371 out of 480 pages.

This is leaving out Matthew, the Pastorals (Timothy and Titus), Hebrews, James, 1 and 2 Peter, and Jude, as of unknown authorship—mostly minor works of the second century, except Hebrews and Matthew, the most commanding book of them all and strangely out of place, we must all feel, with the Pastoral epistles and the second-century Catholic letters, James, 1 and 2 Peter, and Jude. This quite objective comparison brings out sharply the strange improbability that the author of so commanding a book as Matthew, which really never lost its primacy among the Gospels, should have been forgotten! Why? Did the Gospel of Matthew at some time or other slip under a cloud, in church esteem? We cannot learn that it did. From the collection and publication of the Fourfold Gospel about A.D. 125, when Matthew easily assumed the foremost place, probably from its sheer superior religious usefulness, spiritual, moral and liturgical —the Lord's Prayer, the Beatitudes—it seems never to have been dislodged, through more than eighteen hundred years. Even when some manuscripts placed John second, Matthew retained its primacy. Its moral message, too, was unchallenged, with the Sermon on the Mount and the Last Judgment. Its six great discourses offered a presentation of the moral message of the Christian faith unsurpassed and I would say even unequalled in Christian literature, that could not be allowed to lapse or fade from Christian consciousness.

Is it not highly probable that Jesus chose Matthew among his first close followers—he was the first individual he selected—with Isaiah's heroic precedent in mind, and with the intention of binding up his message and sealing it in the minds of his disciples, as Isaiah had so effectually done? We cannot say, in view of what everyone knew had happened in the case of Isaiah, that ideas of this kind were unknown to him. Certainly, in Isaiah's case this plan had had a very definite literary sequel— but no more definite than in the case of Jesus!

Papias' observation about Matthew's connection with the sayings is most naturally understood to mean his "taking down" Jesus' words as he uttered them in Aramaic.

Is Matthew then the secretary, we may even say the recorder of the Twelve, chosen indeed some time before the Twelve were appointed? The four fishermen were told they were thenceforth to fish for men; nothing is said about what Matthew was to do, perhaps because it was so obvious, in the light of Isaiah's course in similar peril. The four were to fish for men; fishing was their trade. Do we need to be told after what Isaiah had said, that Matthew is to apply his skill to its natural purpose, since Jesus' time is likely to be so short? Isaiah's recorders had done their work well; can Jesus find as good a recorder? This is the unmistakable undertone of Mark's crisp narrative. How much Isaiah was in Jesus' mind, Matthew's Gospel clearly shows.

The historical presumption is strongly against the idea that the church within fifty years forgot the name of its chief evangelist. By A.D. 125 or 130 the four Gospels were published together and were then or soon after circulating in a single codex, or leaf-book, the development of which form of book made the effective publication of such a collection possible, in the definite order with which we are so familiar. Some have suggested that that consideration may even by itself have stimulated the codex, or leaf-book, form of book.

I cannot learn that Matthew was anciently ever ascribed to anyone else as its author. The Fourfold Gospel was entitled "The Gospel," each individual Gospel being designated by its sponsor—"According to Matthew," "According to Mark" and so on. And who is so likely to have shown his fondness for numbers and money's use in business and the strange use of fourteens, veiling sevens, and suggesting without mentioning a seventh, as Matthew the tax collector—the man of figures as such, in the New Testament? Surely these staringly obvious considerations must awaken us to the one man among the Twelve who was both man of letters (by profession, he could read and write Greek) and man of figures—arithmetic was the lifeblood of the tax collector. If there were not one apostle proclaimed as such, almost proudly, by the evangelists, would we not have to appoint one ourselves, simply to satisfy these two qualifications?

If we attempt to conjure up another person, gifted alike in numbers and letters for the role of chief evangelist (he does not stand first because of date, but of importance) how can such a person have been anything else than a tax collector? Who else would have known the especial things that he knew and exhibited like accomplishments? The timing of the call of Matthew points strongly to Isaiah's words about his own disciples, and what had come of his action.

If the Gospel is not by Matthew, why was it ascribed to him? He is an inconspicuous figure in the general narrative, except for the story of his call from his tax office to be a disciple, and his prompt obedience. Had his family told Jesus of his awakening interest in Jesus and his message? The circumstance of the subsequent dinner is so vague in Mark as to be variously understood as given by Matthew or possibly by Jesus himself, though this seems unlikely. It may be said that Matthew was the only disciple evidently able to read and write, or at least most likely to have been so. Yet this seems a very slight basis for ascribing the greatest of the Gospels to his hand.

How far back, we must ask ourselves, can the tradition of the authorship by Matthew be traced? The great uncials, of the fourth and fifth centuries are quite explicit about it: Alexandrinus (fifth century), Sinaiticus and Vaticanus (fourth century). The Chester Beatty manuscript (about A.D. 200) has no title, being fragmentary, 18:31-3, 37, 38. The need of an author's name might not necessarily have been always felt until the four Gospels were grouped together, when the distributive "according to" (Greek "kata") was introduced. But this must have been early in the second century, probably

120 to 125; the famous fragment found by C. H. Roberts in the John Rylands Library in Manchester, England, in 1935 is dependably referred to the time of Hadrian, A.D. 117–138, so that 125 to 130 would be a not unnatural dating. But the publication of the Fourfold Gospel as one book is, on other grounds, naturally connected with just this period. And yet the appearance of the Gospel of Matthew within ten years of Mark would have demanded some distinctive name for the new Gospel in an age so insistent upon specific authorship, and in a city like Antioch, then the missionary headquarters of the church.

There are two considerations of major importance which have been widely, indeed one may even say totally, neglected in dealing with the authorship of Matthew. One is the Greeks' exaltation of authorship; they almost worshiped it. The Greeks were averse to anonymity. We shall see how one poem could embalm the name and memory of an author who wrote nothing else that has lived. The bulk of his output meant relatively little to them. If he wrote Greek, and wrote well, it was enough. The whole history of the Greek epigram and particularly its vitality in the first century after Christ shows this. And how can we expect such people to be oblivious of the writer of a book like the Gospel of Matthew?

The second consideration is the unconcern of that Greek world about the sources of a great work and whence they came. The Greeks' interest was in the man or men who had brought it into the Greek world which they knew and understood. Only when it reached Greek form did it have interest and reality and significance for them. Their attitude toward its barbarous sources, as they frankly termed them, was one of disdain. We may dislike and even abhor this attitude, but that does not affect the fact. Their sheer terminology tells the story: Greeks—and barbarians! The author of the Greek Matthew interested them deeply—he belonged to their world; the men who wrote its possible lost sources (if such there were) interested them not at all.

The bearing of these two really well-known Greek attitudes upon the authorship of Matthew is obvious. They support the tradition, in a way that is nothing short of decisive.

4

mark and matthew:
a closer view

IF one takes the Gospel of Matthew and compares it closely with that of Mark, certain striking facts presently emerge. One is that hardly a single incident recorded in Mark fails to reappear in Matthew. It is conservative to say that fifteen-sixteenths of what Mark contains is to be found in Matthew; Canon Streeter estimated it at nineteen-twentieths! Matthew is of course some forty per cent longer than Mark.

On the other hand, much that is said in Matthew cannot be found in Mark. In the field of teaching, this is particularly true. Mark contains much less of Jesus' teaching than does Matthew; Mark presents Jesus as Man of Action, while Matthew presents him as supremely the Teacher. It is a startling fact that if one explores a competent harmony of the Synoptic Gospels, hardly an incident reported in Mark is missing from Matthew; the story of the widow casting in her pitiful offering at the Temple, Mark 12:41–44, is the sole exception, as we have seen. Matthew closely parallels what precedes this incident in Mark—Mark 12:38, 39—and what fol-

40

lows (Matthew 24:1, 2 resembling Mark 13:1, 2 almost word for word). But, of course, Matthew has so castigated ostentation in giving, 6:1–4, that he could hardly make room in his Gospel for an incident that might seem out of keeping with that verdict. And yet Matthew never has the manner of seeming to contradict Mark.

To sum up, Matthew makes use of virtually all Mark has to give, except the woman casting her gift into the treasury, and so commended by Jesus. But Matthew prefers to record the great teaching about doing one's giving in secret, 6:3, 4, and he could hardly use both.

Lake in his *Introduction to the New Testament*, p. 36, remarks, "It is generally conceded that the Gospel according to Matthew provides no trace of the genuine ending of Mark. Matthew 28:16–20 seems to be an editorial addition and it is generally held that Matthew, like ourselves, knew Mark only in mutilated form." Yet it is little short of amazing that, as we shall see, one can actually recover the lost ending of Mark's sixteenth chapter, after verse 8, unmistakably taken over by Matthew before Mark became dilapidated, in completion of its story. But Matthew is in general not at all bound by Mark's order, from which he departs freely. We remember that Peter had nothing to do with that order; Mark had to develop it himself after Peter was gone, so it is no wonder that Matthew found it unsatisfactory. Yet Matthew's procedure is plainly that of a man who has definite information about the order of events, such as Mark did not have.

And if not Matthew, what author of this Gospel can we conjure up? He would have to be a Jew, well equipped also in Greek, with a familiarity with Jesus' teaching that is unparalleled, and one who reported it with an authority no one can challenge. Consider the moral standing of the Sermon on the Mount, and at the heart of it, the Lord's Prayer. Luke also has a Lord's Prayer, but who uses it? Certainly, for Christian devotion, we all follow Matthew, though Luke has a number of parables that are greatly loved and honored—the Good Samaritan, the Prodigal Son, the Pharisee and the Tax Collector. It must not be forgotten that without Matthew we are forced to conjure up as author a vague figure of amazing insight, extraordinarily and unaccountably informed as to Jesus' words and teachings, yet ready to appropriate Mark's modest work and adapt it to the larger purpose that work suggested—a man with an extraordinary vision of Christianity, but unknown to and forgotten by the very Greeks for whom he wrote.

Let us think once more of the action, so meager and yet so significant, at the very beginning of Mark when the forgiving of the paralytic so incensed the scribes, 2:6. Jesus has been teaching the people by the lake, when he sees Levi the son of Alpheus sitting at the tollhouse and says to him, 2:14,

"Follow me!"

What a strange choice! But if we remember Isaiah, what a natural one and what a wise one! Jesus knew the book of Isaiah better than we do,

and this refuge from his enemies would be the one
Isaiah had found and had so brilliantly developed.
Seal the message in a book! Is it not evident that
as the four fishermen are to go on fishing—for men—
the tax collector is to go on taking notes—not of tax
bills but of Jesus' teaching! To the evangelist this
was simply obvious.

As the action develops, nothing much is heard of
Matthew—until the Gospel of Mark bursts upon
the churches. Is not that the fitting sequel to the
call of Matthew, back in the very beginning? Are
we to suppose Jesus had not noticed Isaiah's great
idea of sealing the teaching in the hearts of his disciples until brighter days? But he calls Matthew,
just as soon as hostility begins to show itself; what
reason have we to suppose that he did not have
Isaiah's masterly solution of the same problem in
mind? Let us remember the emphasis Matthew
placed upon Isaiah.

When we remember the Jewish habit of not taking notes (for fear of seeming to rival "scripture"—
"that which was written"), the tax collector, the
inveterate note-taker of Jesus' world, might well
appear a heaven-sent remedy. This is what Papias
was trying to say when he wrote that Matthew
"took down" Jesus' sayings. This accords strikingly
with Matthew's silence throughout the gospel narratives; he was not there to act, or interrogate, but
to record. What reason have we to suppose he
failed in this at first obscure task? Isaiah's disciples
had not failed, and he had them clearly in view.

But while Matthew reproduces in his Gospel

practically all that Mark contains, except Mark 12:41–44, he presents it in an order widely different from Mark's. He evidently considered himself better informed as to the sequence and order of the events of the Marcan narrative than Mark was. And Peter, who was doubtless the chief if not the only source for Mark's narrative, related these things quite incidentally in his preaching without giving any definite information as to their sequence, which Mark had to improvise as best he could. Matthew, or at least the author of the Gospel of Matthew, did not hesitate to rearrange them as he saw fit.

An impression of Matthew's general independence of Mark's order, combined with some very close following of it, can best be gained by a table:

Matthew	Mark
1, 2, Introduction	
3	1:1–11
4	1:12–20
5–7	scattered verses
8:1–4	1:40–45
8:5–13	
8:14–17	1:21–34
8:18, 23–27	4:35–41
8:19–22	
8:23–27	
8:28–34	5:1–20
9:1–17	2:1–22
9:18–26	5:21–43
9:27–31	[10:46–52]
9:32–34	

Matthew	Mark
9:35–10:4	6:6b, 7
10:5–15	6:8–11
10:16–42	
11:1	6:12, 13
11:2–30	
12:1–21	2:23–3:12
12:22–45	3:19b–30
12:46–50	3:31–35
13:1–23	4:1–20
13:24–30	
13:31, 32	4:30–32
13:33	
13:34, 35	4:33, 34
13:36–53	
13:54–58	6:1–6a
14:1–16:12	6:14–8:21
16:13–17:19	8:27–9:28
17:20	
17:22, 23	9:30–32
17:24–27	
18:1–5	9:33–37
18:6–10	9:42–50
18:11–34	
19:1–30	10:1–31
20:1–16	
20:17–34	10:32–52
21:1–27	11:1–33
21:28–32	
21:33–46	12:1–12
22:1–14	
22:15–23:12	12:13–40

Matthew	Mark
23:13–39	12:41–44
24:1–44	13:1–37
24:45–25:46	
26:1–27:61	14:1–15:47
28:1–10	16:1–8

We are struck with the fact that while Matthew adds so much to what Mark has to say of Jesus' teaching, he has little or nothing to add to Mark's account of his movements and actions! But a moment's reflection reminds us that Matthew's records had been of Jesus' teachings, not of his movements about Palestine, of which Mark naturally makes so much; Peter was Mark's chief source, and these short journeys were naturally all planned and arranged through him, as Jesus' head boatman. The difference in emphasis is therefore perfectly in character for each of them. It would seem to become more and more pointless to go poking about for some other author for Matthew, in an age and group so much interested in personal authorship. That the second written Gospel should be anonymous, while the first was not, would be an obvious inversion of historical probability, yet nobody supposes that Matthew preceded Mark! That would at once raise the staggering question, "Why then did Mark leave out the best parts of it?" Alone among the apostles, as far as we can judge, Matthew is the man of books and writing. Some of the others could no doubt do the little writing necessary for their business transactions, and it was probably Aramaic that they wrote. But if anything is to be learned from the accomplishments of the tax collectors of the time, in Egypt, we may suppose Matthew to have had a much better command of Greek than his fellow apostles had need of.

Yet the palpable Semitism usually mistranslated "ears to hear" in Mark 4:9, 23 (its use in 7:16 is probably an interpolation), while imitated by Luke in both passages, Luke 8:8, 14:35, is interestingly corrected in Matthew's parallels, 11:15, 13:9, for he knows that the addition of the infinitive absolute in Hebrew is simply a way of intensifying the imperative—"Let him be sure to listen!" Here his command of Hebrew—and of Greek—is plainly better than that of Mark before or Luke afterward. The "Moth tamuth" of Genesis 2:17—"You shall certainly die,"—clearly exhibits the Hebrew idiom.

Aramaic was not, as far as we know, a literary language in the first century. People did not write books in it, at least none have been thus far discovered. It may be the Qumran caves will disclose some, but that cannot greatly alter the picture. As the Book of Enoch had said, a century or so earlier, there was no place for such composition in Jewish life. The rabbis would not permit the Targums, or Aramaic translations of books of scripture, even of Job, the hardest one of all, to be written down. The *Story of Ahiqar* and the *Life of Darius*, very short books in Aramaic, are clearly translations of narratives of Mesopotamian and Persian origin. We know of no books composed in Aramaic, and while Matthew doubtless told the story of Jesus in Aramaic to

Jews and Syrians again and again, the first Christians were expecting the early return of Jesus to the earth to set up his kingdom and had no time for the writing of books. That was definitely not their frame of mind. "The appointed time has grown very short," I Corinthians 7:29. They must hasten to prepare the world for the coming of the Son of Man. "You will not have gone through all the towns of Israel before the Son of Man arrives!" Matthew 10:23. It was no time for writing books, that was clear, least of all in Aramaic, in which books were practically unknown.

We may also remember the Greeks' passion for taking notes, to which we moderns are so addicted. There is a famous Greek rule or motto, "If you find a saying of a certain Greek philosopher and have no paper, write it upon your garments!" That is, "Above all, write it down; do not trust your memory; commit it to writing!" The Jewish rule was of course just the opposite: Commit it to memory! How Greek had Mark become? Had he adopted this attitude and practice? If so, he may well have been jotting down in his notes particularly good things he had heard Peter say, and have translated them for his Greek hearers in Rome. For the Latin public in Rome was no field for first-century Christianity; it was only among the Greeks there that Christianity found hearers, until almost A.D. 250.

It is Papias of Hierapolis who first mentions both Mark (as the interpreter of Peter, and subsequent evangelist) and Matthew, of whom he says only, "So Matthew noted down the Sayings in the Aramaic language, and everyone translated them as well as he could," into Greek of course. We owe this illuminating fragment to the untiring industry of Eusebius—that amazing man who when called upon to catalogue the library of his patron Pamphilus, not only catalogued it, but read the books he catalogued!—so that in many cases all that we know of those books is what Eusebius remembered from his reading of them!

5

ısaıah and jesus

IN 701 B.C., the prophet Isaiah after a long ministry was seized by King Manasseh of Judah and put to death, tradition says by being sawn asunder! His voice was finally silenced. But Isaiah, who knew the world (he belonged to the aristocracy of Judah) was not taken by surprise by this cruel fate. He had plainly said, probably to his disciples, for he had formed such an inner group to carry on if he were struck down,

"I will bind up my testimony, and seal my teaching in the heart of my disciples. Then I will wait for the Lord, who is hiding his face from the house of Israel; I will set my hope on him!" 8:16, 17.

So it came about, through the tragic foresight of the prophet himself, that when, years after his death, the religious skies of Judah had somewhat brightened, his disciples were able to bring forward the amazing book of Isaiah's preaching—his prophetic oracles, which have claimed such a commanding place in religion ever since. If Isaiah had not gathered a group of disciples about him for companionship and instruction, it would seem clear that the

world would have lost what we know as Isaiah
chapters 1 to 39—that is, all of it that comes from
Isaiah's times, 740 to 701 B.C.—the days of Uzziah,
Jotham, Ahaz and Hezekiah, the kings of Judah.
These chapters amount to thirty-five pages, as compared with some twenty-eight pages of the total
preserved remains of the other three eighth-century
prophets, Amos, Hosea, and Micah combined. The
greatness of the Book of Isaiah even in this short
original form led men in after times to append to it
almost as much more from subsequent prophets—a
clear evidence of the high esteem in which Isaiah's
prophecies continued to be held; if they wanted to
make sure of preserving a prophet's work, they had
only to append it to Isaiah! It speaks volumes.

This procedure of Isaiah's, seven centuries before, had not escaped Jesus. Isaiah's example as a
prophet in perilous and stormy times was not lost
upon him in his silent years, as they are called, before the camp meetings of John the Baptist on the
Jordan had awakened him to his vocation. Jesus
had grappled with the Hebrew scriptures as no man
had ever done, and most of all, one is tempted to
say, with the prophecies of Isaiah.

Certainly, it was when John was delivered up,
that is, imprisoned by Antipas, that Jesus began to
preach, Mark 1:14. And just as clearly, it was when
the Pharisees and the agents of Antipas began to
lay their plans to destroy Jesus, Mark 3:6, that Jesus
retired with his disciples to the seashore, led them
up into a mountain, and chose twelve apostles, to
be with him and to be sent out to preach. It seems

clear that they are to carry on his work if he goes
the way of John the Baptist and is shut up in prison
or put to death; his work, his action seems to say,
must and shall go on.

Are we outrunning the Marcan narrative? No,
look again! The narrative has outrun us! For Jesus
has already chosen four fishermen, Simon and Andrew, and James and John, taken up his abode in
Simon's house, and probably begun to use Simon's
boat as though it were his own. And then one day,
walking along the shore near the town of Capernaum, he sees Levi, the son of Alpheus, sitting at
the tollhouse, and he says to him, 2:14,

"Follow me!"

and Levi gets up and follows him. His call is the
only individual one in the Synoptic Gospels; it immediately follows the first hint of danger—the
scribes' charge of blasphemy—and brings in a man
who aside from being later made one of the Twelve
is never heard of again, whose business as a tax
collector is taking notes.

We sometimes assume that because the first of
Jesus' disciples were unsophisticated fishermen,
they all were. But the remarkable progress of the
Christian mission after Jesus' departure certainly
speaks volumes for the ability as well as the devotion of the men who carried his message, even
though we know so little about their movements
and doings. Paul was not the only intelligent and
able man among his followers; the church at Rome
had reached some size before, or soon after, Peter
arrived there; consider Tacitus' "huge multitude"

(*ingens multitudo*) of them arrested in A.D. 64!
Paul had spent two years there, but as a prisoner.
The mission to Egypt was an important one, difficult as it was, with the anti-Semitic spirit that was
so easily roused there; yet we know nothing of it for
many years. Progress eastward into Parthia and
Armenia was probably the work of apostles, as tradition declares and as we should expect.

I cannot avoid the conclusion that the Twelve
were much abler men than we have been accustomed to suppose, and of course the effect upon
them of listening to Jesus, watching his procedures,
and having the inestimable benefit of asking him
questions simply cannot be described. But a striking
item in the narrative of Mark tells us plainly that
one of them at least was a man of some education,
able to read and write and an adept at figures; in
short he was a tax collector.

Whether the much discussed dinner that followed
Matthew's call—for in the Gospel of Matthew, he is
called Matthew—was in Matthew's house, or in
Jesus' (meaning Peter's) as some interpret it, is perhaps a difficult question, but it seems more likely to
have been the former—the new disciple proud to
show his new master to his friends and declare his
allegiance in the clearest way. In any case it stands
out in the whole story of the choosing of the Twelve;
Matthew is somehow more significant, the evangelist wishes us to see, than most of Jesus' followers.
This was told by Mark years before the Gospel of
Matthew was written, no matter who wrote it.

If, as is not improbable, the fate of Isaiah had

come to Jesus' mind after the arrest and then the execution of John the Baptist (and it was certainly then that he formed his group of twelve apostles), it is not unlikely that he took measures to instruct them, and thus as Isaiah put it, seal the teaching in the heart of his disciples, 8:16. What a mistake to suppose that Jesus was less intelligent than we, and that the fate of Isaiah whom he so regarded was lost upon him! The choosing of the Twelve, so soon after the combination of the Pharisees with the Herodians (the agents of Herod Antipas, John's foe), suggests Jesus' memory of Isaiah's words. What he tells them must be far more than he was giving the people, for it is not too much to say it is meant for later, even posthumous, publication. That had been the method, so brilliantly successful, employed by Isaiah. Is Jesus likely to have done less in this direction than Isaiah had done, and done with such commanding success? And yet Isaiah had had years of public work, where Jesus hardly had had months—or even weeks, perhaps! The flight of the disciples at Jesus' arrest, 26:56, is probably just what he wished and intended; to have them just share his fate would defeat his deeper purpose; his message must survive his earthly career, and it is in their hands that it must survive.

Must not this be the meaning of the extraordinary outburst of Jesus' unmistakably authentic message offered us in the Gospel of Matthew? To an extraordinary degree, it authenticates itself as genuine. Nobody ever spoke like this man! And the Gospel of Matthew in a startling way fulfills that verdict.

Did Matthew gather from the other apostles what he recorded, or was he for some reason particularly privileged in Jesus' teaching of the Twelve? We cannot confidently answer that question, and yet who is more likely to have been thought of by Jesus as a special custodian of his message, in whose heart to seal his teaching?

We can hardly doubt that Isaiah's course in choosing a group of disciples to preserve his teaching until brighter times was back of Jesus' procedure in choosing twelve apostles. Their taking to flight at his arrest was undoubtedly part of their instructions; it would have been a mistake for Isaiah's disciples to join him in prison and martyrdom; they were appointed for another duty altogether. So obviously were appointed the twelve apostles of Jesus; their task was to perpetuate his message, as Isaiah's disciples had done so splendidly, in giving to the next generation the great Book of Isaiah.

But now the time was short, and they gave the world their message orally, repeating Jesus' teaching as widely as they could carry it. And they certainly carried it far and wide. The Jewish war comes on, and results almost in the extinction of Palestinian Judaism. Peter's death in Rome causes his interpreter to write his recollections of what Peter had preached to the Greek believers there, and a copy of it finds its way to Matthew, an old apostle, retired, as we should say, at Antioch. He had supposed the Return on the clouds of heaven would have made such things unnecessary; and yet, think of Isaiah! His teaching had taken shape in a book, perhaps the greatest in the Jewish scriptures. And if there are to be books about Jesus, his *teaching* certainly calls for one. So Mark, depicting Jesus the Man of Action, creates the need for a book about Jesus the Great Teacher, and Matthew writes it. Much of its contents had long since taken shape.

The only problem in all this is, why, with the case of Isaiah and his disciples before them, they had not written before, but the reason is plain enough; they had understood that the time was short, too short for writing books and spreading them. But Peter's sudden and dreadful death had created among his Roman converts a demand for the collection of Mark's memories of his preaching which evidently took the Christian world, such as it was, by storm. The sheer success of Mark's book must have shown the old apostle, Matthew, the response Greek Christianity could make to Christian writing, above all to the kind of writing he had the materials for. I cannot doubt that the thought of Isaiah's disciples and the book they wrote struck him with a new and tremendous force. What a book Jesus' teaching would make! Mark's gospel showed him what a book could mean to the Christian church, and he knew how much greater a book Jesus' teaching could make— of Mark! It seems superfluous to say that the man to write this book must be a personal disciple of Jesus, as Mark was not. Matthew must have awakened with something like awe to the thought,

"Why, this is what Isaiah's disciples did for his memory and message, and this is what Jesus meant us to do!"

6

the ancient tax collector

A S we open the New Testament, we observe that
the editors of the New Testament and its publishers from the early times have made it begin, not
with its oldest documents, the letters of Paul, but
with the four Gospels, and in the forefront of these
from the earliest times has stood the Gospel according to Matthew. But this is an extraordinary distinction for any book. Who was equal to such a test?
And why did the first publishers of the Fourfold
Gospel, away in Ephesus, about A.D. 115 or 120, put
Matthew first? Certainly not because his name carried any distinction; the Gospel made Matthew
famous, not Matthew the Gospel. Still, he was an
apostle, and it was a great thing to have one Gospel
from an apostle's hand. Moreover, it contains more
strong Jewish color in its background than the
others, and the publishers of the four Gospels were
plainly moving from the most Jewish (in background and atmosphere) through Mark—another
Jewish Christian—to Luke, the Greek physician,
and John, the theologian of Ephesus. And the extraordinary religious values of Matthew as a su-

preme source of Jesus' teaching were clear enough
to the ancient religious mind.

And further, they felt the value of an apostolic
author, one of the Twelve. What intimacy and authority that bespoke! This more than outweighed
the unpromising and even detested profession of the
writer—a tax collector!

Approaching the Gospel of Matthew with the tax-
collector author in mind, one might expect an ex-
cess of numbers and of figures, as compared with
Mark and Luke, but this does not seem to be the
case. Certainly, it is not strikingly so. But we remember the famous saying of Horace, in the *Ars,*
that the basis of all good writing is *sapere*—"to have
good taste"—and Matthew had it. Why, it is positively patronizing of us to say so, in view of his subsequent influence. For one single thing, he has
taught the world to pray! We do not pray like Paul,
or Luke, or the Revelation. We find the Lord's
Prayer in Matthew and use no other. The very fact
that we accept his prayer as the authentic one is a
mighty evidence of our respect for him.

And yet, on this sheer numerical matter, Matthew
on examination shows an ease in handling numbers
and figures not unsuitable to his traditional profession. We have seen a startling evidence of this in
his opening paragraphs, where he has actually in-
vested a genealogy with some semblance of interest.
One has only to compare the first nine chapters of
I Chronicles, to see what genealogies tend to become.

Consider also the 25th chapter of Matthew.

There are the ten bridesmaids, five sensible and five foolish. Then follows the story of the man going on a journey, who turns over sums of money to his slaves—five talents, two talents, one talent—very substantial sums, corresponding to five thousand dollars, two thousand dollars, and one thousand dollars. They were to go into business with these sums and make what they could for their master in his absence. And two of them, we are startled to learn, doubled their money! Could a more probable author for this report be imagined than Matthew the tax buyer? For that is what *telones* strictly means—a farmer of taxes, (Oxford lexicon, 1940). And how bitter the rebuke of the man who did nothing at all with his one talent! What did he think money was for? The narrative can have had no likelier recorder than the traditional Matthew. He knew what money was for. We notice, too, that he thinks these small amounts; their master is going to give them larger sums to invest, ver. 21, 23. Surely a more probable recorder of this parable than Matthew the tax collector cannot be imagined. We find ourselves almost wondering whether that authorship was not first suggested by this passage, it is so amazingly appropriate. Yet we recall that it does not stand alone; there is the opening genealogy, to confirm it. Certainly if one demands a signature of Matthew the tax collector, this looks very much like it. What other sort of man in the first century would have imagined this Gospel's way of handling the genealogy and of treating this striking parable, so greatly softened in English by our figurative use of the word "talent," as a native endowment or gift? Luke the physician, in telling this story, instead of talent uses "mina," a coin worth about twenty dollars, and reports each man as being entrusted with the same amount—one mina!

We are struck with several features of the Gospel of Matthew that decidedly favor tax-collector authorship. There is the strange quasi-mathematical feature of the genealogy, which forms the preface. There is an arithmetical subtlety about this which can only be regarded as the literary device of a practiced mathematician. And to judge by the tax papers of Egypt, fractions were a constant feature of their trade, especially duodecimals. Here, however, led by the traditional role of seven in Jewish systems, the seven day week, and the Sabbath of weeks from Passover to the Harvest Festival, not to mention the Sabbatical year, and the Year of Jubilee, after seven times seven years had passed, we are met not by six sevens but by three fourteens, to be followed by a seventh seven. This was evidently the creation of a writer who found delight and even beauty in such elaborations, most of all in the unstated climax, that the Messiah thus became the beginner of the seventh seven, the very height of climax. This certainly looks like the work of a man of figures, to begin with.

Yet most modern interpreters steadfastly decline to see anything of the kind in this highly mathematical beginning. Even the evangelist's studied omission of the last four or five kings to make the second series total just fourteen is lost upon them.

They fail to recognize the touch of the statistician, the tax collector, with his fondness for numbers, and refuse to see that he is simply giving to Jesus a position of supreme climax in Jewish history—the beginner of the seventh seven. That he does not say this in plain words makes it of all the more significance. It is the sign manual of the tax-collector apostle. To have added the Marcan phrase—"The reader must take note of this," as in Mark 13:14 and Matthew 24:15—would have been too obvious. Yet the course of so many modern interpreters shows it was badly needed! We can only conclude that they could never have written the Gospel of Matthew.

Of the duties and labors of a first-century tax collector in Palestine little was definitely known until the discovery more than half a century ago of the Greek papyri in Egypt. A surprising number of these, from Oxyrhynchus and Tebtunis, have to do with taxes of all kinds, and their collection. From Palestine itself nothing of the sort from that period seems to have survived. Yet the two regions must have had much in common in tax administration, although not in the same category under Roman rule, and the study of these Greek papyrus documents from Egypt will throw no little light upon the duties and labors of Matthew the "publican" of Capernaum.

That word itself has had quite a history, as a translation of the Greek word *telones*, which is used some twenty-one times in the Gospels of Matthew, Mark and Luke—three times in Mark, eight times in

Matthew, and ten times in Luke—but not elsewhere in the New Testament.

Matthew is described as a telones, or "tax collector," in Matthew 10:3, and Luke 5:27. In Mark 2:14, Matthew 9:9, and Luke 5:27, Levi, or Matthew, is spoken of as seated at the *telonion*, rendered by the classical lexicon as "customhouse," but by the New Testament lexicographers as "revenue or tax office." It may be thought of, in oriental style, as a building with an open front formed by a counter over which the tax collector did business.

But telones really means a "tax buyer," who bought the right to collect taxes, and probably employed others to do the detailed collecting, making what they could for themselves, as a matter of course. The difference between what he paid the government and what he was able to collect formed his remuneration for his work, and this privilege was sometimes, perhaps often, abused.

The translation of the Greek word telones is an interesting series. Tyndale had said "Matthew the publican," 1525; Rogers, 1537, "publican"; Coverdale, at least in 1550, "the publicane"; Geneva, 1560, "Publicane"; the Bishops', 1568, "which had been a Publican"; 2d edition, 1572, "which [had been] a Publicane"; Rheims version, from the Latin, 1582, "the publican"; King James, 1611, "the Publicane"; but as revised by Blayney, 1769, and now in general use, "the publican."

The Revised Version, 1881, reads "the publican," as does the American Standard, 1901. But the Revised Standard Version, 1946, reads "the tax collector." Yet if we turn to the private translations, in the years since King James, we may trace a definite progression in the use of the word applied to Matthew, in Matthew 10:3. It is still "Matthew the publican" in John Wesley's translation, 1754, and Alexander Campbell's, 1825, and that rendering is revived by George R. Noyes, 1868, and the modern Catholic versions of Father Spencer, 1937, the Confraternity, 1941, and Ronald Knox, 1944. It expands into the gentler, slightly bucolic "tax-gatherer," suggestive of picking fruit or flowers, with Andrews Norton, 1855, Weymouth, 1902, the Twentieth Century, 1903, Moffatt (as one word), 1913, and Montgomery, 1924. Then it assumes the sterner guise, "the tax collector," Rotherham, 1878, (2d edition), Goodspeed, 1923, William Gay Ballantine, 1923, the New World Translation, 1950. But in Frank Schell Ballentine, 1902, it appears as "the saloon-keeper," one who kept a public house. Ferrar Fenton, in 1895, went back to the etymological sense, of "tax-farmer." The latest critical lexicon of the Greek New Testament, Arndt-Gingrich-Baur, reads "tax-collector, revenue officer."

Meantime, Greek papyrus documents of common life had come to light by thousands in the latter part of the nineteenth century, and the numerous private translations of the Greek New Testament that they had stimulated had not neglected the office of Matthew, upon which the papyri had cast no inconsiderable light.

In "The Merchant of Venice," 1:3:48, Shylock's sneer at the merchant—"How like a fawning pub-

lican he looks!"—throws a curious light on what the
poet understood by "publican," a word which had
come or was coming to mean the keeper of a public
house or "pub." This seems to be the only occur-
rence of the word in the plays of Shakespeare.

We are thrown back upon the lexicons and translations of subsequent years, and must consider the
shift in meaning of the English word publican, on
the one hand (it came to mean "a saloonkeeper"),
and more seriously, what the task of the ancient tax
collector was like, a problem on which the Greek
papyri of Ptolemaic and Roman times cast some
light.

Among the Greek papyri in Egypt, which assumed such significance with the discovery of the
Sayings of Jesus papyrus and its publication just
sixty years ago, were revealed a great mass of tax
collectors' papers that must have resembled those
of similar officials in nearby Palestine.

It was in 63 B.C. that Pompey took Palestine for
the Romans, and a generation later, in 30 B.C., that
Augustus took Egypt as the personal possession of
the Emperor of Rome. Of course Egypt had been
largely Hellenized since the time of Alexander. The
two lands came under Roman sway hardly a generation apart, and so their tax systems had in the
days of Jesus' ministry been Roman in Palestine for
three generations, and in Egypt for two, but Greek
in both for three hundred years. They had of course
many points of contrast, and yet in practical ways
they had strong resemblances too, so that we can
learn something of the work of a Galilean tax col-

lector like Matthew from the Greek papyri from Roman Egypt.

It is true, the papyri do not provide us with a complete and systematic scheme of first-century Egyptian taxation, yet they give us numerous glimpses of just the sort of thing that must have formed the daily life and constantly occupied the mind of Matthew, the tax collector of Capernaum.

Tax collecting in the first century at Capernaum, or where the road to Damascus touched the lake, may have been less exacting than it was at Tebtunis, in the Fayum, in those times; yet it, too, probably had its complexities quite as irrational and demanding. The records were doubtless kept in Greek, as they were in Egypt, as a late result or aftereffect of Alexander's conquests. The Greek papyri suggest that the tasks of the tax collector were sometimes far from simple. Indeed these ragged old papyri sometimes take us behind the scenes in a manner almost unbelievable. An interesting glimpse of the strictness with which the Roman administration followed up its officials, in the days when Matthew was a tax collector, comes to us among the Greek papyri from Tebtunis. It is a leter from the *strategus* dated in the ninth year of Tiberius, or A.D. 23, only five or six years before the call of Matthew. Apollonius, the governor of the *nome* ("district" or "county") writes a stiff letter of barely forty words to the *toparch* of the district of Tebtunis, saying,

"Send me at once a supplementary classified statement of payments made, up-to-date, for I shall thus know whether I shall leave you in employment where you are or summon you and send you to the prefect for neglect of the collecting. Farewell.—The ninth year of Tiberius Caesar Augustus, Mecheir (Xandikus) 21." (Tebtunis Papyri, no. 289).

So the Romans in the very days of Matthew held their minor officials strictly to account for their faithful tax collecting. This is not what some historian, ancient or modern, thought about it; this is what a district governor said about it and proposed to do about it, in the days of Matthew the tax collector, only five or six years before Jesus called him to follow him.

Egypt was an older and richer country with a longer history and a more favorable climate than Palestine. We may suppose its tax system, as far as it was an inheritance from Egyptian, Ptolemaic, and Roman administrations, was more elaborate than that of Palestine. Taxes have a way of accumulating. New ones are required by emergencies or new masters, but the old ones tend to stay on. Thus the Ptolemaic taxes of Egypt seem to have lived on into Roman times. As we explore their history we are reminded of a bitter saying from another field of research, "Few die and none resign."

A receipt of 225 B.C., along with two other taxes still unintelligible, mentions the police tax of six drachmas and the tax on horses, one drachma and five obols, meaning doubtless the tax on the horse the taxpayer's military duties obliged him to keep.

Another tax reported from Busiris, in Ptolemaic times at least, was the bath tax, levied upon private

owners of baths, and figured at one-third the pro-
prietor's profits, or 1320 drachmas. The bill goes
on, "He ought therefore to pay for every four days
thirteen drachmas and four obols," and proceeds to
record his daily payments of two drachmas, four
obols, or four and a quarter obols, for a series of
successive days. This was about 245 B.C. There
were apparently no short cuts in the tax-collecting
business; for his payments are painstakingly recorded for the 2nd, the 3rd, the 8th, the 10th, the
11th, the 14th, the 16th, the 18th, the 20th, and
so on, month after month.

The tax on wool, in Ptolemaic times, amounted
to one-twentieth of the wool's value, an instalment
being due every four days, perhaps to make things
easier for the taxpayer, or to keep him from falling
behind, (Hibeh Papyri, 115).

In 1900, Grenfell, Hunt, and Hogarth, in their
volume of *Fayum Towns and their Papyri,* listed
94 taxes they had encountered in the 366 papyri
they dealt with in that volume, the great majority
of them from the first three centuries after Christ,
and some 25 of them concerned with taxes mostly
from the second century after Christ. One, dated
in the second year of Hadrian, A.D. 117–18, was
for no less than seven different taxes which had
been paid by a certain Onnophris, son of Herodi-
anus. One was for the maintenance of the local
guards or police, usually between one and two
drachmas. Another was for *magdola* (watch-
towers), evidently for their maintenance, corresponding to the government guard-boats maintained

by the state along the Nile. As the magdola payment here acknowledged is only two and a half obols, Onnophris has probably paid the bulk of that tax before. Here, as in one other such document, there is an item of one obol for swine tax, but whether this means for one pig or entitled the taxpayer to have a whole herd is hard to say, probably the former.

The range and variety of these small individual impositions are a quaint index of life in the Fayum in the second century, from which time the papyri are for some reason most numerous. Taxes were then as now an absorbing subject, especially of documentation. There was for example the bath tax, for the maintenance of the public baths. This receipt is dated the twenty-second year of Tiberius, A.D. 36, two years after Paul's conversion. There was also the beer tax, usually supposed to be a duty paid by the brewers. One such receipt, in Nero's reign, A.D. 61, acknowledges eight drachmas on account for that year, as well as four drachmas, for the preceding year, also "on account." Another curious and interesting tax, called *syntaximon*, and quaintly rendered "contribution," was designed to distribute among the taxpayers what the state had to pay to maintain the temples. This in some papyri reached 40 drachmas, or even 48, for one whole year. In a Tebtunis receipt of A.D. 28, the twelfth year of Tiberius, a cloakmaker of Tebtunis pays 20 drachmas "contribution," on account.

The contribution tax paid by Theon the son of Mysthes, in A.D. 10–11, the fortieth year of Augus-

tus and therefore in the childhood of Jesus and
the evangelist, was in three instalments, aggregating
44 drachmas and 6 chalci. As this amount is also
found in receipts for this tax from others, it was
doubtless the regular amount of it.

Weavers paid a regular tax in the first century,
in monthly instalments apparently aggregating 38
drachmas. One such receipt has been found, for
the second year of the Emperor Nerva, A.D. 98.

A tax duly paid on the sale of a cow in A.D. 134
perplexes us, as no amount is given, but as the cow
brought 44 drachmas of silver, the tax was probably
the regular ten per cent.

The poll tax varied with the status of the taxpayer, but also with the locality. In Thebes it varied
with the locality—10 drachmas, 16 drachmas, 24
drachmas. At Oxyrhynchus some people paid only
12 drachmas, but in the Fayum, frequently 20
drachmas, and one taxpayer as much as 40. It has
been conjectured that the higher tax was paid by
Egyptians, the lower by Greeks or Greco-Egyptians,
except the *catoeci* (settlers)—who were exempt.
They were the military colonists settled in Egypt
after the Greek conquest, and apparently their
descendants.

Another frequent tax, especially important in
Egypt, was the *naubion* tax, based on the area of
land held by the taxpayer. The naubion was a cubic
measure of soil to be dug by the subject in building
dikes or canals; he escapes this work by paying
this tax. It is levied upon the holders of various
kinds of land. It varies from 100 to 150 copper

drachmas per *aroura*. (The aroura-measure was 100 cubits square.) The size of the naubion (the body of earth to be removed) has been found to have been the cube of two "royal cubits," or supposedly one yard, that is, it was about one cubic yard of earth—very much the modern unit for such operations. Rather than engage in such backbreaking manual labor, people of any substance would of course pay the tax substitute. There would be little room for such operations, we may suppose, in Palestine, and there the Egyptian naubion tax was presumably unknown.

It is clear that in Egypt at least, and no doubt to some extent in Galilee, every parcel of land had a history which was reflected to some extent in its taxation. The tax collector must know these histories. Nor was his task lightened, from the modern point of view, by his invariable way of keeping his numerator one. Certainly, the duties of a tax collector in Egypt were a complicated business, to say the least, and matters of exemptions and exactions did not simplify it. One cannot help recalling the three fourteens at the beginning of Matthew; to a tax collector, a statistician by occupation, reducing the traditional kings' list to three fourteens would have been a joyous relaxation.

Another tax item was the physicians' tax, which was sometimes paid directly to the physician to be supported and paid in kind, not cash. In a papyrus of 248 B.C., a military settler from Cyrene pays directly to the doctor, whose name was Eucarpus, four drachmas as physician tax for the year, though he really pays it in produce—ten *artabas* of *olyra*, or rice wheat, also mentioned in the Iliad as food for horses, and sometimes identified with the modern durra. The settler, a private, undertakes to pay the doctor this amount in the month Daisius or forfeit to him two drachmas an artaba, or twice the normal value of an artaba; so ancient is government medicine.

The manner of recording fractional amounts of artabas is not without interest. One plot of Crown land was described as arouras 3 1/2 1/4 1/8 1/64 in extent, or as we would say 3 57/64 arouras. This plot was figured as paying a rent of 5 1/3 1/15 1/375 (5 151/375) artabas but he does not find it necessary to add the fractions up; these men must have been lightning calculators, to say the least. This may show the lengths they were prepared to go in their tax calculations.

The sales tax was a substantial item—ten per cent on the sale price of a house at Tebtunis. This tax had developed under the Ptolemies, and this rate was sustained under the Roman Empire. A helpfully itemized tax receipt of A.D. 192, the thirty-third year of Commodus, records the payment made by Harmiusis the son of Ploution, who has been away for some time and now pays back taxes for some four years.

It is indeed not less than amazing that a duodecimal system was actually employed for some purposes. If this seems incredible, consider a letter about seed grain, from the fourth year of Antoninus, A.D. 140–41, Tebtunis Papyri II, 341, where it is pointed out that the artaba is usually divided "according to a duodecimal system, 1/48 1/96 1/192, etc." Lest this appear incredible to the modern decimal mind, consider the actual reading of the letter: the land involved is 3 1/2 1/4 1/8 1/64 (that is, 3 57/64) arouras, which paid a rent of 5 1/3 1/15 1/375 artabas of sifted wheat, which we would call 5 151/375, but they did not add fractions. Certain allowances which are faithfully computed and reported but do nothing to simplify the transaction, we may disregard.

No! Let us rather include them, so that we may glimpse for a moment the sort of thing Matthew's life consisted of. For this property carried an additional rent item payable in beans to the amount of 1/2 1/45 1/300 of an artaba, which we would instinctively total, (but the ancients would not) at 473/900 of an artaba of beans!—Such were the sums that were passing forever before the tax collector's weary mind. They must have almost counted the beans!

The tax on sacrificial calves (A.D. 208) has been much discussed. Was it paid by the priests to the state? More probably it was paid by the person offering the calf, who thus sacrificed not only the calf but paid a tax of 20 drachmas to the state for the privilege. The priests however were also called upon to pay the government one-tenth of their profits from such offerings, Tebtunis Papyri II, p. 101. But we cannot say that this condition extended to Palestine and Galilee.

The sheer mathematics of taxation was then, even

as now, puzzling. A report on grain revenues, about A.D. 190, mentions some perplexing amounts, which made no difficulties for the tax collectors. Amounts are involved of 4742 1/48 1/96 artabas of wheat, 355 1/2 1/3 1/12 1/48 1/96 artabas of barley. We observe that as soon as the computer gets to ten or tenths, he shifts to duodecimals. But fifths and tenths could not easily be added to thirds and fourths. Some scribes, however, preferred multiples of eight: 1/8, 1/16, 1/32. Papyrus 356 presents some staggering series: Wheat, artabas 4787 1/2 1/3 1/12 1/48 1/96; Barley, artabas 266 1/3 1/12 1/48 1/96. Such constant experiences made the tax collector perfectly at home with figures and some kinds of fractions.

Dr. Breasted has pointed out in his history of Egypt that the Egyptian scribes could operate only with fractions having "one" as the numerator, and all other fractions were resolved into a series of several, each having one as the numerator. The only exception was two-thirds. (*History of the Ancient Egyptians,* p. 40.) This curious mathematical limitation survived in the tax figures of the Ptolemaic and Roman times.

We moderns in fact have not gone entirely decimal. Consider our divisions of time; twelve months in the year, twelve hours in the day from midnight to noonday, and twelve from noon till midnight; sixty seconds (five times twelve) in a minute, sixty minutes in an hour. We even divide the circle into 360 degrees! We are not entire strangers to the duodecimal view of things ourselves, so we may

not altogether look down upon the ancients as they
wrestled with the task of formulating a system for
the facts of everyday experience.

In the second volume of Tebtunis Papyri, dating
from 231 B.C. to the third century after Christ,
the index lists one hundred and eleven different
kinds of taxes in vogue in Greek and then Roman
Egypt between 231 B.C. and A.D. 224, a period
of little more than four and a half centuries, cen-
tering about the active life of Matthew the apostle
and his contemporaries. Certainly, Egypt was not
Palestine and their taxes doubtless displayed sharp
variations; but the Palestine list may well have been
quite as long and varied as the Egyptian, which
covers not all of Egypt, but a very limited area of
the Fayum. Some such varied range of tax problems must have occupied the working days of
Matthew the tax collector, and probably in Greek,
too, for in administration Palestine was still using
Greek, as Egypt was. A hundred and eleven different kinds of taxes would soon give a man a legal
if not a liberal education, though it might not of
itself fit him to write the Gospel according to
Matthew that we know. Matthew must have learned
a high degree of tax reporting and recording in his
profession. He also developed a considerable vocabulary; McNeile has shown that Matthew's Gospel
employs a hundred and ten words not found elsewhere in the New Testament—a statistic I had
myself arrived at before observing it in his commentary.

These varied examples of ancient tax collectors'

activities are not gathered from Palestine, it is true, but they give us light on the ordinary routine doings of similar officials in nearby Egypt under the Romans, in ancient times, and very much such labors and calculations must have occupied the tax collector Matthew up to the moment when Jesus called him to be his disciple. It can hardly be thought more likely that it was quite another man, but with a similar background, that took up the task of the evangelist in Antioch about the year A.D. 80. This is not to say that Matthew originated those parables of high finance, but rather that beyond the other apostles, Matthew the ex-tax collector, from his experience and observation, understood them and so reported their meaning.

One of the most striking of the papyrus discoveries is the place of shorthand in ancient business and official life. Grenfell and Hunt in 1904 published a papyrus from Oxyrhynchus bearing strongly upon this matter. It was a deed of apprenticeship for a slave named Chaerammon to be taught shorthand for two years by Dionysius the son of Apollonius, a shorthand-writer. It was understood that in that length of time he might be expected to master it. The payment was to be 120 drachmas. So in A.D. 155 the teaching of shorthand was a recognized business, even in a remote upcountry town like Oxyrhynchus, which is on the Bahr-Yusuf, not the Nile. Chaerammon is to be able to write fluently and read faultlessly. It is generally understood that Paul's letters were for the most part dictated to amanuenses who took them down in shorthand and then wrote them out: that is the obvious meaning of the conclusion of Galatians, which Paul adds in his own hand to what he had previously dictated to the professional letterwriter.

A study of tax collectors in Egypt in New Testament times and their ways of computation begins to throw some light on the singular way in which Matthew's Gospel begins, with its strange sequence of three fourteens. If the tax collectors of Egypt (and presumably of Galilee) were habituated to a duodecimal system of computation, what more natural than for one of them to advance to a quartodecimal grouping, such as is found in Matthew 1:1–17? The editors apologize for these fractional eccentricities by charitably noting that "the presence of these curious fractions of the artaba which is usually divided according to a duodecimal series, 1/48 1/96 1/192 etc., is due to a deduction having been made for cleaning the wheat." At all events it is good to know that it was a deduction.

So we have bathed our spirits for a while in some such mundane activities and problems as must have occupied the tax collector Matthew all his waking hours, until Jesus so dramatically said to him,

"Follow me!"

and in two words (one, in Aramaic) brought him from utter obscurity to the high places of history.

7

was the apostle
the evangelist?

THE opening lines of the Gospel of Matthew present a genealogy of Jesus from Abraham down; through David and the royal line of Judah; then after the Exile through Zerubbabel down to Joseph, "the husband of Mary, who was the mother of Jesus called Christ."

Such sources as we possess for the genealogy in the Old Testament, primarily I Chronicles 1–3, offer an interesting comparison with this concise listing. It is more literary in form than Luke's longer list, which works back from Joseph all the way to Adam, "the son of God." Yet Luke's concise businesslike list of seventy human ancestors reaching back to Adam is in strong contrast to Matthew's, which traces Jesus' line through Solomon, Rehoboam and a dozen other kings of Judah who do not appear in Luke's list. Nor do they agree at all after the Exile.

It is clearly the purpose of Matthew to glorify Jesus' ancestry by listing a series of the kings of Israel and then of Judah through which it might theoretically be traced. He has even held this royalty section of his list to fourteen names, followed by fourteen more, thus reaching the end after twenty-eight generations from David to Jesus, while Luke lists a succession of forty-one ancestors for the same period. For the earliest period of Matthew's list, Abraham to David, of fourteen generations, Luke has thirteen.

Matthew's list is evidently controlled by his artistic purpose to group the ones he lists into three fourteens, so that Jesus begins a fourth fourteen, or rather, since Matthew's three fourteens amount to six sevens, Jesus begins a seventh seven, a position of obvious numerical climax. This may fairly be taken as a mystic numerical way of exalting his position; he began the seventh seven. I cannot help feeling that here at the very outset it is the veteran tax collector who virtually identifies himself by this mathematically artistic way of introducing Jesus.

The earliest Christian attitude toward book-writing was doubtless very much that of contemporary Judaism, which held that in the Jewish scriptures they had all the writings necessary to religion. The fallen angel Penemue was guilty of instructing mankind "in writing with ink and paper, and thereby many have sinned from eternity to eternity and until this day. For men were not created for such a purpose, to give confirmation to their good faith with pen and ink." (Enoch 69:8–10)

Even this admonition was hardly needed by Christian believers, for they held that the time was short and Jesus would soon return upon the clouds of heaven. It took a major disaster, the execution of Peter, the chief of the apostles, to alter this attitude at least to the extent of recording his gospel story, as one of his Greek interpreters had been wont to translate it from Peter's Aramaic preaching into the Greek speech of the Christian believers in Rome. The result was the first book to appear in the speech of plain people. This was done about A.D. 70, for the destruction of Jerusalem is strikingly reflected in its discourses. They are vividly remembered because they have so very recently been fulfilled. And so in Rome, the Gospel was written, in Greek, by Mark, and in no long time a copy of it found its way to Antioch, the great Christian center of the day, and there met the eye of the aged apostle Matthew, whose days of active missionary travel were presumably over. To him it very soon suggested the better book that might be written. And is it not obvious that he found guidance as well as suggestion in the Gospel of Mark?

The appearance of the Gospel of Mark, in Antioch, brought there by Greek believers from Rome, perhaps, reminded Antioch anew that the years were passing, and while the time of Christ's coming tarried, there was a Greek world to be saved. Certainly the arrival of the Gospel of Mark in Antioch led to the writing of the Gospel of Matthew. For Mark provided the author with much of his narrative and awakened Antioch to the needs of the immediate present for a full written account of Jesus' teaching, as well as his doings. To such a work, a definitive Gospel, some Christian leader in

Antioch now set his hand. And who but an apostle
could hope to step in and undertake to improve
upon a book that owed virtually everything it contained to Simon Peter, the chief of the apostles?
Even for Matthew, it was a serious test of what he
had to offer. But with Matthew it was no mere
afterthought; it is obvious that the writer of Matthew had spent years in the recollection, contem-
plation, and formulation of Jesus' message, as he
alone of the Twelve could have remembered and
even recorded it. He is great enough to have no
hesitation about appropriating such narratives as
Mark preserved—he leaves hardly anything out—
but he writes to supplement Peter's recollections
with a statement of Jesus' *teaching* that has been
the wonder of the world ever since. The result was
what was virtually a new book, one of the most
tremendous value and significance.

We are struck with the fact that the basic meaning of *synegrapsen,* the word Papias uses of Matthew's writing, is "write or note down," as a
stenographer takes down a dictation; this is its
first meaning, in the great Oxford lexicon of 1940.
And what more natural than that this converted
tax collector should take down Jesus' religious utterances, when he signaled for it, or when Matthew
himself thought what was being said especially
novel or striking? This is certainly not putting too
much into the duties of Matthew, in view of his
profession and his very dramatic call, in the light
of Isaiah's fate and what his disciples did to preserve his message, with such great success.

Papias also recorded some extraordinary statements of Jesus about future grain and vegetable production, which have always seemed wildly extravagant to his readers in ancient, medieval, and modern times, but which in our own period of agriculture simply melt into the light of common day! Perhaps Jesus did, as Papias says, anticipate something of the vast surpluses we know so well. The only reaping implement in those days was a sickle. Think of it, not even a scythe! The earth was fertile enough, but they had no idea how to reap its products. Not so many years ago I have seen the sickle in serious use in reaping wheat, in more than one modern European state. I hope it is now obsolete, but I greatly fear it is not!

We are asked to believe that the actual author of the Gospel of Matthew has been forgotten. And yet Mark, a very minor figure as compared with the author, was not forgotten, and writers of Greek books and poems were faithfully remembered. Matthew is so much more impressive than Mark that it would certainly seem that a public that so faithfully remembered Mark would never forget Matthew. Why, the Greek Christians proceeded swiftly and cheerfully to forget Mark and to turn with one accord to Matthew, or at least to the Gospel that bore his name. The publishers of the Fourfold Gospel, A.D. 115–20, could not find one complete copy of Mark—nor has one ever been found!

For did the leading Gospel, as we have all come to consider it, ever bear any other name? We can-

not learn that it did; and no other explanation of
this fact is as natural and likely as that Matthew
was simply the name of its Greek author. We have
seen how steadily that rule prevailed in the Greek
book world. The plain and obvious sense of the
name is unmistakably that the Greek Christian
public in which the Gospels made their successive
appearances, named them in the unfailing Greek
fashion from the particular men who put each of
them into Greek. This cannot be too often or too
boldly stated, for it is being almost totally forgotten.
So we must repeat that the Greek reading world,
in which and for which the Gospels were written,
had a definite and instinctive attitude about this
matter which admitted of no compromise! Some
scholars speak and write as though it were a casual
matter, depending on the personal attitude of this
or that Greek author. But the evidence is quite
otherwise; let us review the list: the Septuagint
coolly credits the Torah of Moses to its seventy
Greek translators ("the Seventy" is in Greek
Hebdomekonta, in Latin *Septuaginta*) and then
goes blundering on to credit them with the Greek
translations of forty or fifty subsequent books of
Hebrew literature, as they passed into Greek, and
joined the collection! And in the first century, Mark,
Matthew, Luke, Paul, Clement, Hermas—every one
named for its Greek writer unless the exception
is Matthew!

In such a literary world to name a gospel for
some half-forgotten (and from the Greek point of
view, half-civilized) document thought to underlie

it, such as the supposed Aramaic sayings of Jesus, would be altogether unlikely. What the Greek wished to know was, "Who put this record into Greek and so introduced it to the attention of civilized men, like myself?" That was the way the founders of Christian literature—in Greek—felt and operated. Mark, the first book of Christian literature—called Mark, because he had written it, in Greek! Matthew, the second such book, written in Greek and so accepted by Greek readers! Luke, the third such book, written by Luke, Paul's beloved Greek doctor! He accompanied it with a second volume, the Acts of the Apostles, telling of the spread of early Christianity to its establishment in Rome. The letters of Paul were now collected and published in two volumes, that is, scrolls— *volumen* means a scroll, or roll. They were welcomed by the Greek reader, for they were written in Greek and were of surpassing interest, in themselves and for their light on religious problems. Then the letter of Clement, Bishop of Rome, to the Corinthians (I Clement). Then the *Shepherd* of Hermas, a Christian of Rome, at the very end of the first century.

This is substantially the list of Christian books written in Greek in the latter half of the first century. And they are every one of them named for their Greek authors—unless we must except the Gospel of Matthew! That, many scholars say, is not called by the name of its Greek author but by that of a man who wrote an Aramaic account of Jesus' teachings. But that is precisely what the

Greeks did not do—name a book after its barbarian sources.

It is clear that to name a book from some remote and, to the Greek mind, outlandish source that lay back of it was not at all the Greek way of doing, and Matthew is a contribution to Greek literature. Mark was an attempt to present the Gospel to Greek readers, and within a decade the Gospel of Matthew frankly sought to do it better and brilliantly succeeded. Matthew's contribution to this success is acknowledged. The only question is, Was it made directly, by Matthew expanding and enriching Mark, or indirectly, by some unknown combining Mark with a Matthew document? But in that case, would the Greek editors or publishers have called it by Matthew's name? No, not if their procedure with Mark, or even Moses, is any criterion. They called it Matthew because he was the man responsible for its Greek dress, which was of course their chief concern. This is the clear evidence of Mark, Luke, and John. These men, at home in Greek, had written these books in Greek, for the Greek public. And why judge Matthew by a different and highly artificial standard, unsupported by the Greek way of rating books, at least from the times of Philadelphus and the makers of the Septuagint in Greek—the *Hebdomekonta,* the seventy translators of the Book of Moses? They did not call their Greek version *Moses!*

This very obvious fact has been too often overlooked in dealing with the authorship of Matthew, a task in which we are asked to turn away from all previous parallels in ancient Greek book titles and reverse their evidence. Philadelphus' translation committee had calmly divided the Hebrew scroll of the Torah into five scrolls of convenient Greek length, giving each a suitable Greek title—Genesis, Exodus, and so on, and calling the collection the Seventy. In very much the same way, one historic form of the English Bible is loosely spoken of as "King James" and a recent revision of it is called the "R.S.V."!

There is above all the improbability that in the Greek atmosphere in which the Gospels grew up, the name of the author of the leading Gospel should have been overlooked and forgotten. We know the names of the other early evangelists—Mark, Luke, John—and why not Matthew? The manuscript tradition—what the ancient copies said—is in no uncertainty about it. It must be remembered that with the written Gospels we are not in a Jewish atmosphere, which did not recognize personal authorship; the epigrams teach us that among the Greeks a tiny poem of a few lines could give a man literary immortality. So highly did the Greek world value individual authorship.

The question that arises is, Has the Gospel of Matthew ever been ascribed to anyone else, or has a nameless figure, deemed more likely than Matthew to have written it, ever been conjured up or described?

It is obviously very natural for Matthew, if he is the apostle and so in close touch with all these events he takes over from Mark, to rearrange them in accordance with his own personal recollection, which might well be more correct than Mark's conjectural reconstruction of their sequence.

Another objection to Matthew's authorship is the evident use in the Gospel that bears his name of one or even two minor documents later used by Luke, which were unknown to Mark or at least were unused by him. But obviously Mark did not possess complete information as to all that had happened, and Matthew may well have welcomed them as supports or supplements of his own personal recollection of what had occurred fifty years before. I have known modern writers on events largely within their own knowledge, when called upon to record them a generation later, to seek and use additional material from other informants when it promised to supplement or even modify their own recollections. There is nothing improbable in such a course; to deem it so is to conjure up for the writer of our Matthew an unnatural attitude, blind to inquiry, and indifferent to improvement. Why suppose that he confined his researches to Mark alone?

For the old apostle who has been repeating Jesus' teaching as best he could for fifty years—the most literate of them all—and who now combines his recollections or even his records of it with the narrative at last published by Mark, is more likely than not to have taken advantage also of what these floating fragments of history and tradition had to offer. He uses Mark; why not them? Their inclusion by Matthew, so far from contradicting his authorship, may just as well point directly to it, and we must ask why it would be easier to understand if someone other than Matthew wrote our first Gospel. Matthew's large use of Mark shows at once that he does not intend to confine himself to his own personal notes and memories.

Indeed this is precisely the difficulty found with Matthew; he is too important! But such literary methods cannot succeed. They imply that only un-important people can write books, but as soon as they write them they become important—and are at once rejected from the role of author. Is it not plain that such preconceptions defeat themselves? Matthew was not important—he was almost a lay figure—until he writes a Gospel! But then he is at once rejected as an author simply because he is too important. The first Gospel must, it is assumed, have been the work of somebody who was never heard of! This sort of literary historical method simply defeats itself. Writing the Gospel made him too important to have written it!

What will such methods of criticism make a thousand years from now of the massive writings of Herbert Hoover and Winston Churchill? It will of course decree that they are not from the hands of these world figures at all, but are the work of hacks, writing at their orders! For that matter, what do such critics think of the historical writing of Julius Caesar, on the Gallic War? They have attacked it, and the later work on the Civil War, the latter with some success. But be it noted, there is no disposition to ascribe the Gospel of Matthew to *Jesus!* Only to some obscure follower of his, otherwise unnoticed, who shows such insight and information that his creators are at a loss to explain who he was and what became of him, in that Greek world of high regard for authors.

That Matthew's name, as we are asked to believe, was given this Gospel because he wrote, not it, but a supposed Aramaic source of it, I find doubly improbable, for the Greeks, as we have seen, while they did call books by the names of the men who wrote them in Greek, did not name them after the writers of their barbarian sources, as the Greeks considered them.

Against this background of Christian literature down to the year A.D. 100, the title of the Gospel of Matthew obviously means written in Greek by Matthew, an apostle who as a tax collector, must have known Greek and how to write it, and who was very strikingly publicly chosen by Jesus in the fifty-ninth verse of the Gospel of Mark (2:14)— one-eleventh of the way through it! In fact, Mark has hardly begun, when he introduces the fifth disciple, Matthew the tax collector. The occasion for it was the rising peril from the scribes, who charged Jesus with blasphemy, and that meant death by stoning!

Papias' observation about Matthew's connection with *The Sayings* (*logia*), is naturally understood to mean taking down Jesus' words as he uttered them—a service which in the light of Matthew's call, in Mark 2:16, forcibly recalls Isaiah's use of his disciples. His further statement that each one

translated them as best he could seems to refer
primarily to the Twelve, who would have access
to them (they doubtless remained in Matthew's
hands) and if they wished to use them in Greek
"translated them as best they could." I cannot see
that any published book of these sayings is indi-
cated, as is often assumed.

Is it not obvious that a Greek atmosphere that
would have called the Greek Old Testament the
Septuagint after its first seventy translators into
Greek, and the earliest Gospel "according to Mark,"
although he had derived it all from Peter, and the
whole of plane and solid geometry "Euclid" after
the man who had organized and recorded it in
Greek, would also have called the second Greek
Gospel "according to Matthew," not because he
wrote one of its Aramaic sources (if he did), but
because he put the whole into Greek? In the first
century no other explanation would be adequate.
In consequence the titles of the four Greek Gospels
reflect the four men who were responsible for their
Greek forms. This rule did not last indefinitely, but
in the first generation of Christian literature it
clearly prevailed. The four Gospels bear the names
of the men who wrote them in Greek.

The tenth chapter of Matthew, the second of
Jesus' six sermons in this Gospel, is certainly the
fullest and clearest body of directions for the Twelve
in their labors that the Gospels contain, and it is
natural to suppose that they reached the evangelist
through one or more of the apostles—unless he was
an apostle himself, which is the most natural expla-

nation of all. Even so, some may wonder at their inclusion, except as essentially the fundamental instructions of the apostles as missionaries, and hence appropriate to all early missionaries of the Cross.

Only once, 10:2, does Matthew call the Twelve "apostles." They are simply the twelve "disciples," 10:1; 11:1; or "the Twelve," 10:5. He does not dwell upon their apostolic rank or dignity. But no other Gospel gives such space and detail to their instructions; in Matthew's chapter 10, they fill all but four verses, or thirty-eight. No other Gospel gives such a discourse, or instructions of any such length to the apostles. This is in fact a commanding feature of the Gospel of Matthew, and pointedly suggests its apostolic origin. Who else would know so fully what the duties and functions of the twelve apostles were to be?

The presence of this discourse of instructions to the apostles in chapter 10 is very obviously an indication of apostolic authorship. The writer must either have been present among the apostles or have obtained this detailed information from someone who was. It comes very near being a definite claim of apostolic authorship. The complete naturalness with which this is done disarms objection. But if the author is not an apostle (namely Matthew), the question must at once arise, How did he obtain this private information? Or was it made up conjecturally by the supposed nonapostolic author? I cannot find that the holders of this view face this problem; they seem to think their non-

apostolic pseudo-Matthew got this information indirectly from some apostolic source, perhaps church
tradition. Much of it is paralleled in Mark, chapters
3, 6 and 13, and much is found also in Luke 6, 10,
12 and 21. Jesus may of course have said some of
these things to larger audiences at various times,
and the apostles must have repeated some of them
on numerous occasions; in fact every line of the
instructions is paralleled in Mark or Luke, or both,
at least once except 10:5, 8b, 23 and 41. Yet Mark
and Luke give little prominence to the discourse
as such; Mark devoted 6:7–13 to it, and Luke 9:2–
6. But many sayings which Matthew refers to this
discourse appear here and there in other connec-
tions in Mark and Luke. The sending out of the
Twelve has no such place or emphasis in Mark or
Luke as in Matthew. Here it is made the occasion
of one of the six great discourses that distinguish
the Gospel of Matthew. Certainly its inclusion as
a complete discourse, comparable in length and
vigor with most of the other major discourses in
Matthew, must strike the reader as highly appropriate, if the writer of the Gospel is indeed one
of the twelve apostles to whom the discourse is
addressed, 10:5. They are specified as apostles only
in one place, 10:2, looking on as it clearly does to
the list of the apostles to be given in verses 2–4.
The other references to the Twelve in connection
with their immediate mission, 10:1; 10:5; 11:1, do
not speak of them as apostles, but as disciples, or
as the Twelve, a singularly tactful course if the
writer is himself an apostle. He leaves the reader

in no uncertainty as to who were addressed in these instructions, but does not harp upon their apostolic dignity.

If we scrutinize the contents of the Gospel of Matthew, we find little difficulty in discerning the marks of the apostolic tax collector. The opening lines of the Gospel, reducing Jesus' ancestry to three groups of fourteen generations each, so that he obviously begins the seventh seven, though this discovery is left for the reader to make for himself, come very near being the sign manual of the man of figures, the statistician! What other solution presents itself? The writer's enjoyment of figures is apparent, in some of the narratives he has included in his book. The story of the Workers in the Vineyard might confuse a different hand, for some work twelve hours, some nine, some six, some three, some one, but all receive the same wages, 20:1–16. Only Matthew records this parable, which still perplexes some people. The Parable of the Ten Bridesmaids and their lamps, Matthew 25:1–13, is not reflected in the other Gospels. The Parable of the Talents, great sums of money, is reduced in Luke to the minae. Matthew describes the sums to be handled as substantially five thousand, two thousand, and one thousand dollars; Luke reports them as twenty dollars each! Which sounds more like a man of monetary experience? But in the Unforgiving Debtor, Matthew 18:23, we are really in the world of high finance, for the slave's debt is ten thousand talents, or ten million dollars! The debt due the slave from his fellow slave was a hundred shillings, but fairly worth a hundred dollars in value. This startling story is found only in Matthew.

It is easily assumed that the twelve apostles were rude peasants or plain workingmen, and some were. But being with Jesus was a rapidly transforming experience, not only in character but in intelligence. With him they began at once to breathe a larger air, and to view what they saw about them in a grander perspective. Of this there can be no doubt. Nor is Matthew a distinguished figure, authorship by whom would give added importance to a book. On the contrary, it might well repel the reader. Who wants to read a tax collector's book?

Learning has pretty well settled down to the belief that Mark wrote the Gospel that bears his name, and Luke the two-volume work known to us as the Gospel of Luke and the Acts of the Apostles; John is just as clearly the work of the man who wrote the letters of John, the great Elder of Ephesus, or as the Greek manuscripts of the Gospels usually style him, John the Theologian (Theologos), for theologian he certainly was. He set the new faith on the theological rails on which it was to run for a full thousand years.

If tradition has been vindicated in these three identifications of authorship, the fourth Gospel (actually the first) is left in an isolation that is highly provocative. Why was ancient opinion wrong about it, and it alone? Matthew is such a completely lay figure in early tradition; he never offers any remark or performs any act, nor does he even ask a question. He would seem to have been a silent auditor. And the Gospel attributed to him from the earliest times is the commanding source of Jesus' teaching unto this day. This is a literary paradox which calls for more searching scrutiny than it ordinarily receives.

Is not this the very link that Papias supplies, when he says that Matthew "took down the sayings"? It is a singular thing, as we reflect upon it, that the call of Matthew is so dramatically emphasized, not only by Jesus in making it, but by Mark in relating it. We cannot escape the impression that it is the only individual call of a disciple in all the Synoptic Gospels! It evidently so impressed Peter that he related it in his preaching in Rome, where Mark not only translated it into Greek for Peter's Greek hearers there, but after Peter's martyrdom wrote it down in his recollections of Peter's account of Jesus, Mark 2:14.

It is evident that the household of Alpheus was an early nucleus of Jesus' followers at Capernaum; think of Mary, and how she stood by Jesus in the fearful tragedy in Jerusalem, until they laid him in his tomb! A wonderfully courageous and devoted woman! And consider her sons; James, Joses, and her stepson Matthew, two of them apostles! Is it fanciful to wonder whether Matthew had not already developed a strong interest in Jesus' work and message, when Jesus gave him that most dramatic call, right there at his office; and Matthew as promptly responded? Certainly, they were not total strangers. Jesus must have had some special service in mind for Matthew; Matthew evidently did not disappoint him, for Jesus later included him among the Twelve. In view of Isaiah's splendid example with his disciples, and the farsighted use he made of them, and his memorable words, 8:16, "I will bind up my testimony, and seal my teaching in the heart of my disciples, then I will wait for the Lord," we may fairly expect Jesus not to hesitate when his own work, only begun, was imperiled. And as we look back upon the situation, Matthew seems the logical man to record Jesus' message, as Isaiah's disciples had done for Isaiah. Jesus made no mistake in choosing Peter and training him. And what about Matthew? Remember this was well before the calling of the Twelve, as Mark tells the story; the call of Matthew is in Mark 2:14; the call of the twelve apostles is a chapter later, in 3:14. In the Gospel of Matthew, Matthew is called in 9:9, but still before the choosing of the Twelve, in 10:2.

Are we not struck by the reticencies of Matthew? He does not explain the three fourteens of the genealogy, or his own call, so early and so abrupt. He is never heard of again except in the lists of the apostles; why then is his call so featured in Mark—and Matthew too? We have to wait for a solution, or a hint of one, until Papias—and he is generally misunderstood! But he reveals Matthew's chief function among the Twelve; he was the secretary, the recorder, such as Isaiah had had to such good purpose.

Jesus' teaching in the Gospel of Matthew clearly culminates in the picture of the Last Judgment, with its presentation of a moral ideal so far in advance of all others. This is the moral climax of the Gospel, shared with no other. Certainly the recorder of it was a man of extraordinary moral understanding. He began his account of Jesus' teaching with the Sermon on the Mount, and he concludes it with this incomparable picture of the Last Judgment. How tremendous to represent Jesus as the judge! But how far more tremendous his standard of judgment:

"In so far as you did it to one of the humblest of these brothers of mine, you did it to me!"

The Gospel reaches its moral climax in these tremendous words. Is there anything like it in the Bible —even in Matthew itself? You would think it difficult for a writer who has begun with the Sermon on the Mount to rise higher still, to a final climax, but the author of Matthew is fully equal to it. His climax is here, in the tremendous canvas of the Last Judgment.

It is no mere Galilean peasant that records these scenes and sayings that still search men's hearts with such amazing power. Association with Jesus had had its effect; it still touches and stirs our hearts; but who of us reaches such heights?

It is a remarkable fact that the language of this scene is to a great extent colored by the language of the *Testaments of the Twelve Patriarchs,* that strange document written about 100 B.C. that Grosseteste brought to England in the thirteenth century. For it was Robert Grosseteste, the great Bishop of Lincoln, who obtained from Greece a

Greek manuscript of this strange work, which is now in the university library at Cambridge. It is of the tenth century, but eight other Greek manuscripts of the work are known to learning, as well as more than a dozen Armenian manuscripts of it, and even a Slavonic version, in two forms. Its striking resemblances to the phraseology of the gospel account of the Last Judgment may be in part explained as reflex influence of Matthew's language upon manuscripts of the older document, which may have been to some extent brought into agreement with Matthew. But what remains shows that Jesus' language in the parable, as I should call it, is in part colored by his acquaintance with the *Testaments,* the original form of which he may very well have known. Its attitude toward forgiveness reveals one of the noblest teachings of pre-Christian Judaism, but this attitude toward forgiveness had been lost in the subsequent development of Pharisaism, in the century and a half that ensued before the appearance of Jesus. Elsewhere in Matthew, 5:14, "Ye are the light of the world," reminds us of "Ye are the lights of Israel," *Testament of Levi,* 14:3, but here the contrast is even greater than the resemblance. Perhaps the most striking resemblance to Jesus' language in Matthew 25:35, 36, is in these lines in the *Testament of Joseph* 1:5, 6:

> I was beset with hunger, and the Lord himself
> nourished me; . . .
> I was sick and the Lord visited me;
> I was in prison, and my God showed favor
> unto me.

These are of course literary allusions to Joseph in Egypt, but the *Testaments* may well have been familiar to Jesus and the evangelist. There is doubtless literary influence here, but the touches that Matthew here owes to the earlier Hebrew book are used with far greater effect in the Gospel than they were in the *Testaments*. It is interesting to observe that the literary horizon of Jesus and his circle was not confined to what we know as the Old Testament.

Matthew was by no means the last man to think of Jesus in such terms of climax, and as the beginner of a new era. Four and a half centuries later, a Roman abbot Dionysius, called Exiguus—the Small, or Humble—introduced the dating of events, no longer from the founding of Rome, but from the birth of Christ, and thus inaugurated the Christian Era. We can imagine how congenial that would have been to the evangelist Matthew! Nor is this inclination without contemporary echoes; great men still so regard him, though they put it in modern ways:

"The life of Christ," said Professor Whitehead, "has the decisiveness of a supreme ideal, and that is why the history of the world divides at this point of time!"

8

the background
and approach of matthew

THE remarkable picture of the call of Matthew,
Mark 2:14, Matthew 9:9, has an overtone
which must not be missed—it implies that the reader
will recognize him as the chief recorder of Jesus'
sayings. We may suppose that early Christians
heard that with their first oral instruction in Jesus'
teachings. We must remember that the tax collector
seemed to the general Palestine public to be per-
petually writing things down; that was his role.

For the tax collector was the one figure in ancient
Palestine who wrote everything down. That was his
distinctive job. And now the Greek papyri have
come along to underscore this impression. Why is
so much made of his calling and profession in the
Gospel accounts of his call? The only other call
recorded in the Synoptics is that of the four fishermen on the lake, perhaps because Jesus added to
his call,

"I will make you fish for men!"

What he would do with a tax collector who spent
his life writing down his notes was plain enough.
And is it not clear that this is what Papias meant

when he said that Matthew "took down"—*syneg-rapsen*—Jesus' sayings? That is the first meaning given for the word used, in the Oxford lexicon of 1940, "write or note down," and it is the word used by Eusebius in recording the remark of Papias on the role of Matthew. This is the clear implication of the call of Matthew. If Jesus was going to train the four fishermen to fish for men, he was clearly going to give Matthew sayings and teachings to record. That was so obvious to the ancient writer that he did not think it necessary to say it! But what else would Matthew be called for!

There is therefore no difficulty in supposing that Matthew the Apostle in his own lifetime of preaching had formed a way of setting forth Jesus' teaching. He even committed it to writing and used it with the Greek and Jewish inquirers of Antioch. The sudden appearance there of the Gospel of Mark in Greek, about A.D. 70, presenting as it did Peter's point of view, must have interested and stirred him profoundly; it was so telling a story of Jesus' work and its climax. But its defects were obvious; it began with virtually no intelligible introduction and missed Jesus' role as the world's great Teacher. It must be given a suitable introduction, and Jesus' teaching must be made its commanding feature. Without leaving out anything in Mark worth mentioning, Matthew proceeds in an order of his own, to correct its glaring defects and make of it what has always remained the supreme statement of Jesus' teaching! It was so immediately convincing that it soon overshadowed Mark completely,

(Would this have happened if it was not by Matthew?) and only the broad vision, a generation later, of the Ephesian publishers who saw the Gospels as allies, not rivals, saved Mark from oblivion. Even *they* could not find a complete copy of Mark to include in their Fourfold Gospel collection, it had fallen into such neglect. Matthew had clearly so surpassed it as to drive it out of circulation.

And there can be little doubt that one of Matthew's points of superiority to the all but anonymous Mark, was its author's name. For after all, who was Mark? A newcomer in the Christian enterprise and no apostle at all.

But it was the apostles whom Jesus had chosen and trained to carry on his work. If his expected return was still further to be deferred and books were to be written in preparation for it, it should be done by his chosen disciples, his apostles; think of Isaiah! That was the feeling of posterity, and it may well have been that of the apostles themselves, certainly of the most literate of them all.

If Matthew had made notes from time to time of things of especial interest and importance that Jesus had said, he would naturally have done so in Aramaic, the language Jesus spoke and they all used. Unlike Jews in general, the tax collector took written notes and preserved them. That was characteristic of tax collectors. When the Christian group fled to Antioch before the Roman legions, Matthew may well have taken these notes with him, indeed he would certainly have done so; he had repeated them so often in his twenty-five years of missionary work that he could not forget them. Presumably these were the sayings of which Papias had heard at Hierapolis. In Antioch, of course, his public was largely Greek, and he naturally translated the sayings into that language as he had occasion to use them, or unwritten things that he simply remembered. This is doubtless the background of Papias' remark, and of Matthew's wealth of other material with which he later so enriched the written Gospel in Greek from the hand of Mark. Judging from the tax-collector papyri from Egypt he must as a tax collector have used Greek as his official language, in his communications and records. As we have seen, the word Papias uses of Matthew's writing has as its first meaning in the lexicons, "to write or note down"—precisely the sense we should expect of Matthew's original "noting down" of striking things he heard Jesus say. Indeed, Jesus' selection of him as one of his first disciples clearly had this very aptitude in mind, in view of Isaiah's conspicuous example, Matthew's professional fitness for the task, and his own evident personal peril.

The confusion in the first chapter of Mark extends through verse 13; some scholars even fail to detect the effort in that verse to reflect Psalm 91:11–13, no matter how faintly. It was soon felt that there must be a stronger, more arresting approach to the great theme, that would make a specific appeal to the chief religious groups of the day—Jews, Astrologists, Stoics—so out of the Old Testament histories and the memories of gospel beginnings the Christians had brought with them from Jerusalem to Antioch, Matthew composes this approach.

Jerusalem may have been a narrow scene, but probably at the very outbreak of the war with Rome, A.D. 66–70, the church had forsaken the doomed city and fled northward to Antioch, already the basic center of the Greek mission. Yet the Jews, too, were strong and numerous in Antioch, where many of them had taken refuge, and the current conflict with Jewish ideas and morals strongly colors Matthew's rendering of some of Jesus' discourses, particularly chapter 23.

Astrology was so potent a religious force in the first century that Tiberius spent the middle years of his life studying it on the island of Rhodes. And even today, a great metropolitan daily in this country (along with two hundred other such papers) devotes some seven columns a week to its doctrines.

As for the Virgin Birth, third item in this extraordinary introduction, it was a favorite feature of Stoicism, for its heroes were usually believed to be sons of Zeus by special generation. Even in the very years when Matthew was being written, about A.D. 80, a great Stoic, Epictetus, was saying of one of its virgin-born heroes, Hercules,

"But none more his friend than God, for which reason he came to be considered the son of God, and so he was! It was in obedience to him that he went about purging away injustice and violence!" (*Discourses*, 2:16).

So Epictetus, at the very time Matthew was being

written, was allegorizing the virgin birth of Hercules! So strong was the virgin birth idea even in pagan minds, at the very time of the writing of the Gospel of Matthew. In this remarkable threefold preface or introduction, the evangelist invites the interest of Jews, astrologers and Stoics in the personality of Jesus.

But an omission of Mark's struck the new evangelist as demanding improvement; that was the *teaching* of Jesus. Mark has faithfully treated his movements and his activities, but how meagerly Jesus' teaching has been presented—no Sermon on the Mount, no Lord's Prayer, no Beatitudes! As Matthew saw it, Mark's presentation of Jesus' teaching was totally inadequate, and to this task he set his hand with the power and skill of one with whom Jesus' message had been his chief concern for fifty years. This was no subject Matthew could work up on the spur of the moment. One even dares to wonder whether it was not for some such service that Jesus had chosen Matthew, a most improbable candidate for apostleship, one would suppose, and yet if Isaiah's example had any interest for Jesus, it must be entertained. Isaiah had chosen one disciple, at any rate, who could record his messages, and after the storm was over and the time had become ripe for it, he had put forth his message to the Jewish public. This was what had made Isaiah the commanding figure we all know.

With the fate of John the Baptist staring him in the face, must not Jesus have sought just such a man as Isaiah had? And Matthew, with his books and figures was the man, if his heart could be touched.

Tax collectors were adept at taking notes; in Greece they even used shorthand. We may fairly imagine that Matthew would not wait fifty years before setting down in writing much that he had heard from Jesus—not of course for publication; Christians still believed that the time was short and the end was at hand. Yet time went on, and whatever local mission field Matthew was given was evangelized. Matthew, now an old man and veteran of missionary campaigns, sees the Gospel of Mark, at Antioch; and the book, good as it is, points him on to the better book that can and must be written, the story of Jesus' *teaching*.

Yet some would say, some other believer in Antioch composed our present Gospel on the basis of the two sources, naming the new book after the author of its Aramaic source. But such a method of crediting authorship would have given Mark to Peter, its Aramaic voucher and source; yet its Greek publishers actually gave it to the man who wrote it down in Greek, and that was Mark. Would not the same procedure inevitably have assigned what we know as Matthew to the one who wrote the book they knew, in Greek, from no matter what sources? The Greek public was interested in Greek authors, and the names they applied to books then were those of the men who wrote the Greek forms of these books that they knew and read—Mark, Luke, Paul, John. Even Peter's name they did not directly connect with the Gospel that derived its material from him, and he was the chief of the apostles, as all agreed. It was Mark, his translator into Greek, whose name was given by unanimous consent to the record of Peter's memories and his preaching. Why, even the Pentateuch, put into Greek, tradition has it, by order of Philadelphus, 285–246 B.C., as we have seen, was given the name not of Moses— the books of Moses—but of its Greek translators, who were according to tradition Jewish elders seventy (or seventy-two) in number; in Greek it was the *Hebdomekonta,* in Latin, the *Septuaginta,* as if the Seventy were its authors! And from the Greek point of view they were! For the Greek reader, these strange old writings can hardly be said to have existed until some divinely gifted man translated them into Greek, the language the reader could understand! We are reminded that probably in the same reign of Philadelphus, Euclid became a synonym for geometry and has remained so for more than two thousand years. So the Septuagint became the Greek name for first the Torah, the "five books of Moses" as they became in Greek (they were one in Hebrew), then as the rest of the Old Testament passed into Greek, for the entire Jewish scripture. So deeply disposed were the Greeks to name a book or a literature for the man or men who put it into Greek and from their standpoint brought it into existence.

Viewed in this way, the Gospel of Matthew can hardly have been given his name from a supposed source used in its composition; the Greeks cared more for the individual who put it into Greek, whatever his sources might have been. Nor is it easier to conjure up some supposed basic document in Matthew and connect that with the apostle Matthew, as the explanation of the giving of his name to it, widely as this is assumed. It is hardly a Greek way of procedure and we are now, as we have just seen, beyond the merely Jewish sphere; consider chapter 23! No, the name of the Gospel according to Matthew must be understood by Greek standards. It is a little like what happened to geometry, which had been developed by a number of mathematical thinkers, Eudoxus, Theaetetus, and others—when under Ptolemy Philadelphus, a Greek geometer named Euclides systematized its elements in Greek, and lo and behold, geometry, plane and solid, became "Euclid," unto this day!

The effort to push Matthew back into the position of a mere source of his Gospel thus loses sight of what was happening in Christian literature— Mark, Luke—and had long been happening in Jewish Greek literature—the Septuagint, whose name had been so extended as to cover a host of religious works written long after the time of the Seventy, back in the old days of Philadelphus. In the presence of this great development, religious and scientific, and its nomenclature, there is no difficulty in recognizing in the Gospel of Matthew material from the apostle's own hand combined with material which came to him formulated in Mark, though in an order which he could not accept. Indeed, his transpositions of Mark's material at once suggest that he has been a partaker in the events he records, and that he feels competent to reshape as well as to enrich the Marcan narrative. It is to be noted that Luke takes over Mark's units in Mark's order, which is just what Matthew declines to do. Matthew thought he knew better.

But whether Matthew had indeed kept a record of Jesus' sayings (logia) as Papias seems to say, or not, his own Gospel proved the richest and most powerful presentation of them the first century affords, and this fact strongly supports its ancient ascription to Matthew the apostle, especially in view of the Greek habits of nomenclature, as exhibited in Mark, Luke, and the Septuagint.

We must not fail to notice the existence of shorthand in Greece and Rome in the first century before Christ. In Greece it had long been practiced, and more than one system was in use. A competent tax collector may well have been acquainted with it, for use in his duties, but of course we cannot claim that he was. We must only note that the ancient world was not in all respects so antique as one may be tempted to suppose. In other words, we cannot safely assume that Matthew had no knowledge of shorthand, when at least two Greek systems have been discovered, besides one in Latin. With the latter, Cicero's famous secretary Tiro is closely associated, though not necessarily as its creator. But Greek shorthand manuals have been discovered and published by H. J. M. Milne of the British Museum in 1934, on the basis of nine Greek papyri of the third, fourth, and fifth centuries. While these do not come from the time of Christ, they reflect a developed and established system, in basic elements quite as old as Cicero and his ingenious secretary. They may fairly be said to suggest that such practices were by no means unknown in the time of Christ. But of course Jesus spoke in Aramaic, and no Aramaic shorthand system has yet been found. Mr. T. C. Skeat, Deputy Keeper of Manuscripts in the British Museum, kindly calls my attention to a recent history of shorthand ("Geschichte der Kurzschrift") published by Arthur Mentz in 1949.

Let us put together these facts for what they may be worth, and for their possible, or even probable, coherence. Isaiah, confronted by a hostile king, takes the precaution of gathering a group of close disciples about him and giving them his best instruction. They survive him and in due time, when the personal danger is past, bestow upon the people of Judah what he has taught them. We know it as Isaiah 1–39. Its authors (being Jews) were anonymous.

Jesus, confronted by a similar peril from another king, Antipas, gathers a group of disciples about him, for closer instruction, and among the first of them is Matthew, a tax collector, skilled in writing Aramaic, the language they all spoke, and Greek.

Matthew accordingly takes down, in Aramaic, many very important utterances of Jesus, as we may well surmise. As a tax collector he was accustomed to take down a great many tax details, like the tax collectors in Egypt, whose ways we know so well.

Years after, Peter's martyrdom creates a demand in Rome for some record of what he had been teaching his Greek converts there, and one of the viva voce translators of his Aramaic preaching into Greek writes down in Greek much that he remembers of it.

This first Christian book is welcomed in Rome, and copies of it go as far as Antioch, then the chief center of the Christian movement. There one falls into the hands of the aged Matthew, a conspicuous figure, we may well believe, in the church. He is fascinated by the book, like everybody else. Yet he soon sees how much better a book may be made of it, with the aid of the teachings of Jesus, which he had so long preserved and taught.

So arises an enlarged and improved Gospel, rich, as Mark's was not, in the teachings of Jesus. What should it be called? Obviously, as Mark's was called the Gospel in its first line, the *Gospel*—and of course, *of Matthew*, since Mark's was popularly known as *The Gospel*. Now if not before, *of*, or *according to*, *Mark* must have been added to the title, in popular use. But the palpable superiority of Matthew's book soon caused Mark to begin to decline in influence, leaving Matthew the *supremes* story of the ministry and the teaching of Jesus.

9

the SECRETARIES
of the prophets

THE secretaries of the prophets! Had Jesus one?
The question is almost sacrilegious, and yet
Isaiah had clearly come into Jesus' mind when
Herod's minions and the hostile Pharisees began to
turn their attention from John to Jesus. He was
plainly to be the next. No wonder he calls twelve
disciples to be his inner circle, his apostles, to carry
on his work when he is gone! This fact overshadows
the Gospel of Mark from the beginning of the third
chapter. The shadow of the Cross already falls upon
the page.

Jesus looked to his disciples—his apostles—to carry
his memory and his message past his murderers and
into the future. Think of the Last Supper! That is
the keynote. Paul strikes it in I Corinthians 11:24:
"Do this in memory of me!"

And Isaiah had his secretaries—his disciples, he
calls them—to write down his great utterances, and
keep them safe till Manasseh's persecution had
spent its force and a new king was on the throne.
We do not know their names; only Jeremiah's faithful Baruch, we must suppose, rescued the writings

and the utterances that survived that prophet's ministry and final flight to Egypt, and disappearance there. The men Isaiah found to be his disciples and recorders were no insignificant servants; they were strong and able men; the Book of Isaiah is in no small degree their monument.

One of the apostles, the first of them to be individually chosen, as Mark tells the story, was the tax collector of Capernaum. The sequence of events here is obscure, but we learn eventually that he was the son of Alpheus, whom we know also as father of another apostle, James. While Alpheus is nowhere called a disciple, his household was extraordinarily loyal to Jesus, and we are given the impression that he was, presumably, a well-known disciple himself. Matthew was his son, probably by an earlier marriage.

Among the disciples, the presence of a man with plenty of writing experience, Greek as well as Aramaic (he would interview the taxpayers in Aramaic, and write up his reports in Greek), is a fact of great importance. This is seen to be in striking accord with noteworthy features of the Gospel of Matthew. It begins with that strange introduction of Jesus, as the climax figure of Jewish history—the beginner of the seventh seven from Abraham. That this is not stated but left to the reader to compute clothes it in slight mystery but makes it all the more emphatic; on the face of it, he seems to begin the fourth fourteen, which of course means nothing. We are in the company of a writer perfectly at home with figures, even delighting in them. This trait as we have seen reappears in many items—the laborers in the vineyard, some working twelve hours, some nine, some six, some three and some one—but all paid the same wages! Only Matthew records this transaction. The slave forgiven by his royal master a prodigious debt of ten million dollars—and yet unwilling to forgive his fellow slave a debt of a hundred! No one else records these parables. The three slaves given various sums to go into business with, while their master is away—one five thousand dollars, one two thousand, one one thousand. Luke has a similar story, but with him the amounts are very small. Luke talks of minae, each worth some twenty dollars, but Matthew talks of talents, each worth a thousand dollars! In Luke each man receives the same amount, one mina. It is clear that Matthew has no dread of large sums. A study of the more than a hundred words peculiar to Matthew's Gospel looks in the same direction.

Is it not clear that Isaiah's disciples were not involved in his cruel fate, but escaped, as he wished them to do, and carried with them the priceless records of his prophecies, to hide and protect until a better day dawned for their proclamation? And as for Jeremiah's faithful secretary Baruch, when Jeremiah disappears from history in the confusion of the escape to Egypt, he is left behind, or gets back, evidently with his own records of the prophet's preaching and vicissitudes. We have no reason to suppose Jesus oblivious of such clear historical precedents for his own situation, or disinclined to follow the courses taken so successfully by these ancient prophets, for the more ancient of whom at any rate he showed the most signal esteem and even reverence.

The names of Isaiah's secretaries we do not really know, but Jeremiah's Baruch is a fairly familiar figure. His secretarial character shines through the narrative parts of the book of Jeremiah, 32:14, 16; when he bought the field of Hanamel, at Anathoth, he confided the deed to Baruch, to deposit in an earthenware jar, for security, 32:12–14. A little later, 43:6, the mass flight of the dispossessed Jews to Egypt did not fail to take Jeremiah and his right hand man Baruch along with it into Egypt. In 45:1, Jeremiah gives further prophetic dictation to the faithful Baruch, still a model of courage and fidelity, even in a strange land. We cannot doubt that it is to him and such as he that we owe the fulness with which Jeremiah's utterances and experiences are recorded—at almost twice the length of the authentic records of Isaiah.

Even the earlier prophets had their attendants— their servants, or even slaves, who sometimes played a significant part in their operations for good or ill. Elisha began as the one who "poured water on the hands of Elijah," and in turn was waited on by Gehazi, of tragic memory. His successor was more faithful, 2 Kings 6:17. One great difference between the so-called "literary" prophets and their predecessors is that the latter found no recorders, until Hilkiah the priest, while cleaning up the neglected temple for King Josiah, found the Book of the Law in the House of the Lord, and in a sense began the formation of the Old Testament, 2 Kings 22:8. It was the work of one of the secretaries of the prophets, working in secret in Manasseh's cruel reign, to rewrite the old law in the new prophetic spirit, and it became the nucleus of the Jewish scriptures.

It was certainly no new thing in Jewish history, if Jesus, faced by the peril of a speedy end, sought the services of the tax collector, with the pen of a ready writer, to preserve what he could of the message Jesus knew he had for his time and world and all that were to follow. And this is clearly what the much discussed words about Matthew taking down Jesus' sayings, had reference to.

It was a sudden and unforseen contingency that led to the writing of the first Christian book, the Gospel of Mark. It was Peter's martyrdom that precipitated its composition. With Peter cut off by a cruel and violent death by crucifixion, at the height of his work in Rome, his Greek converts so much missed his daily sermons on Jesus and his life and words that Mark, Peter's leading Greek interpreter in his Aramaic preaching, was driven to write down all he could remember of it, and so arose the Gospel of Mark. It was primarily meant for Peter's Greek auditors in Rome, but soon copies of it reached Antioch, the new center of the Christian movement after the fall of Jerusalem and its destruction, A.D. 66–70.

A full generation had now passed since the Crucifixion, and the first vivid expectation of Jesus' return had grown dim. The appearance of the Gospel of Mark and the welcome it received awoke the church leaders to the service Christian books in Greek might render.

But the old apostle there in Antioch soon saw the larger possibilities of this new gospel type of literature. Not only does it seem to him to demand an adequate introduction, suited to its time and public, but its crying defect is in the matter of Jesus' teachings, some of the greatest of which are entirely absent from it.

And who but an eyewitness back in that first generation of gospel writers, would have felt qualified to rearrange Mark's recollections of Peter's preaching as Matthew has done? Mark of course made no pretense of having witnessed what he related, and Peter had not set up the order of the events he recorded; they were simply told incidentally in his preaching as the occasion demanded. And Luke, the other user of Mark in making a gospel, did not presume to rearrange them. A glance at any competent harmony of the synoptists, in Greek or English, will soon reveal that. Luke's appropriations from Mark appear in Luke in Mark's order, but what Matthew takes over is freely rearranged, a fact which makes Luke the delight of the harmonist, but Matthew his despair! No contrast could be sharper. This clearly means that the writer of the Gospel of Matthew felt that he was better informed about the sequence of gospel events than Mark had been, and also that the sequence of the teaching mattered more than the continuity of the action!

Matthew had doubtless for years been relating the teaching of Jesus as he remembered and indeed probably had recorded it—he was a tax collector, and was accustomed to take careful daily notes and to write down his records. Is is not obviously for this function that he is appointed, so abruptly and so early in the narrative of Mark, at the first threat of peril? What is he to do? Why, of course, what he had always done—record everything. The ancient tax collector was the inveterate note-taker of antiquity. He left nothing to memory, but wrote everything down. The papyri have illustrated this abundantly, as the pages upon pages of their Greek remains show. And this is why Matthew virtually disappears from the narrative after his call; he was the secretary, taking his notes. He performs no striking act, asks no questions, plays no leading part; that was not his role. He merely records. To the ancient reader who knew tax collectors and what their chief activities were, this hardly needed saying. It was self-evident. And this is why the call of Matthew which appears to us so abrupt and detached, seemed to them self-explanatory. Jesus' teaching from now on had a recorder, as Isaiah had had, long ago, and that was what had saved Isaiah and his message from oblivion. Can anyone suppose Jesus and his circle, with their great regard for Isaiah, failed to see this?

10

fIRST CENTURY GREEK
LITERATURE

IT is sometimes lightly assumed that Greek literature as a current activity was extinct by the time of Christ or at least virtually inactive, but this was far from being the case. The Liddell-Scott-Jones Greek-English lexicon of 1940 records no less than fifty Greek authors who are referred to the first century after Christ. This does not include any New Testament writers, nor any whose periods of activity overlap the first century B.C., or the second century A.D. These, if included, would add about half as many more to the list, while the Christian writers would add half a dozen more.

Nor were the works of these Greek writers of the first century of little significance in literature. We observe among them the first novelist, surely a fruitful literary line never more prolific than today. His name was Chariton, and his novel was the romance of Chaereas and Callirhoe. The finding of a second-century papyrus of a considerable part of this novel in Karanis, an obscure village in the Fayum, and another in Oxyrhynchus, in Upper Egypt, suggests that this romance was probably written in the first

century after Christ. If to the invention of the novel
we add Philo in Alexandria and the Book of Wis-
dom, and Josephus at Rome, together with the first
Christian Gospels, at the other end of the scale, the
literary value of the first century becomes simply
overwhelming. And yet these manifest facts are for
the most part lightly passed over, if not altogether
ignored. We say nothing of Paul's letters, since
they were, in intention, simply personal communications. Yet imagine a century in which mere personal
communciations attained such stature!

We may think first of Onosander, a first-century
philosopher who wrote a commentary on Plato's
Republic. This has not come down to us, but Onosander's military book, the *Strategicus,* on the duties
of a general, has survived. It was dedicated to Q.
V. Nepos, consul in A.D. 49 and legate of Britain. It
is said to have been "the chief authority for the
military writings of the Emperors Maurice and Leo,
and Maurice of Saxony expressed a high opinion
of it."

Demetrius' work *On Style* is now assigned to the
first century; he is believed to be the friend of
Plutarch who taught Greek in York in A.D. 80. His
book is still a significant work in the field of rhetoric.

We are tempted to think of the evangelists as
voices cryng in the wilderness, and in a sense they
were, yet those were the days of Plutarch, Epictetus,
Josephus, not to mention many lesser Greek writers
whose works have survived eighteen centuries, and
are with us still.

There was also the little book *On the Sublime,*

formerly assigned to Longinus of Palmyra, but now referred to the first century and still acknowledged to be a classical piece of literary criticism.

Then there is Dioscorides, with his monumental work on *Materia Medica,* listing six hundred plants and drugs useful to medicine, and until three centuries ago still considered the most valuable guide to such plants and drugs—a landmark in the history of botany and pharmacology.

In poetry there were the Epigrammatists, thirteen of whom flourished in the first century, with a total of 164 epigrams still extant, some of them of the most touching feeling and beauty. Antiphilus of Byzantium is represented by no less than 49, from this first century, but Ammianus, Eutroclus and Pinytus are also remembered and included, although they have left only one epigram each! What could better show the Greek regard for authorship in the first century? A single tiny poem of half a dozen lines would embalm an author's memory forever! That was the Greek literary world of the first century, and it was the world in which Christian literature arose.

Where did they live, these first-century Epigrammatists? Byzantium, Sardis, Alexandria, Miletus—all over the Greek world. This was its literary atmosphere. But if a single epigram of a few lines was enough to preserve a man's name and memory forever, what about a book like the Gospel of Matthew? Would such a world let its writer's name perish? Considered from the Greek side, such a thing is impossible. It is even inconceivable!

We have seen that the collection of the Greek epigrams, the *Anthology*, has among others from the first century after Christ one only from Ammianus, one from Eutroclus, and one from Pinytus. Yet they sufficed to keep these names from oblivion, in the pages of the *Anthology*, for nineteen hundred years. The single epigram of Pinytus that has survived is only two lines long:

> The tomb holds the bones and the dumb name
> of Sappho,
> But her skilled words are immortal!

But they won him a place in the *Anthology*. And are we to suppose the Gospel of Matthew was not equal to preserving the name of its writer? Or are the advocates of that position unaware of these plain contemporary literary facts?

Were these names and poems really worth this literary immortality? The Greeks of the first century thought so, and so did their successors in the safeguarding of their literary heritage in the *Anthology*. And what are we to think of the attitude of the Greeks of the first century toward the Gospel of Matthew? In bulk, and in value to religion and morals it was worth a thousand epigrams, at the very least; would they be careless of its authorship and negligent of it? Would the first-century Greeks, for whom it was written, have no interest in its real writer and be indifferent about whose name was given it? Was their behavior, so scrupulously careful about a thousand epigrams, not all of them masterpieces, limited to these minor poets? Of course not!

It was a deep basic devotion to Greek literature and its makers. Many such Greeks became Christians; a few years later, Christian literature in Greek was a torrent! The Christians virtually took over the Greek language; Christian literature even in Rome was Greek, to the middle of the third century. And would this Greek concern for authorship not embrace a book of the obvious power and elevation of the Gospel of Matthew? Remember we are no longer in the Semitic realm of anonymity; with the Greeks, literature and authorship had become personal. To put it another way, an age capable of producing the Gospel of Matthew was sophisticated enough to remember who wrote it. These are considerations so widely neglected by writers on Matthew that it is worth-while to recite them.

It is a striking fact that the Gospel of Matthew originated in Antioch, then the most thriving center of the Christian movement, foremost in the missionary enterprise and other respects; there their name, for instance, was first invented, evidently by their opponents: "It was at Antioch that the disciples first came to be known as Christians," Acts 11:26.

And it was at Antioch that the Gospel of Matthew was written—in this center of the Jewish controversy, which was also the source of the Greek mission; in Harnack's phrase, the first fulcrum of the Christian movement. Antioch was its stage; and it was here that the Gospel of Matthew made its appearance. How then could it have emerged obscurely, anonymously? These things were not done in a corner, but on the most conspicuous stage of Christian doings of the day. The possibility of Matthew's appearing anonymously, at just that time and just that place is unthinkable. They were Greeks, too, born and brought up with a great regard for authorship; when one saw a book, his first question was, "Who wrote it?" And with a new gospel, this demand would be intensified. They already had one, the Gospel of Mark, or the Gospel. And now another? By whom, pray? That question was inevitable, and as its dramatic and moving contents developed before the reader, it was multiplied tenfold; they must know the writer of this startling, even amazing book. That he should have passed from sight uninquired for is simply unbelievable, particularly in the Greek Antioch of the seventies.

But Matthew would not want to be passed by and left unknown and forgotten. For he felt that he had been doing his master's will; it was for that that he had written this religious masterpiece; has it an equal in the wide world? He had done it as an apostle of Jesus, seeking to do his will and carry on his work. And how well he had done it! Then why be silent about it?

And yet how often we moderns find ourselves thinking of first-century writers as voices crying in the wilderness! Not at all! That was a vigorous and even a brilliant literary world. Christian literature did not arise in a vacuum, though some writers treat it as though it did. Consider Luke's quotation from Aratus, about 300 B.C., which he puts into the mouth of Paul speaking to the Athenians. Perhaps

Paul did use it, but certainly Luke did, and that shows that Greek-speaking Christians in the first century had other horizons, some of them, than the Old Testament. Certainly the verse in Aratus is not unworthy of Paul's attention:

> Zeus fills the streets, the marts,
> Zeus fills the seas, the shores, the rivers!
> Everywhere, our need is Zeus!
> We also are his offspring!

Just as certainly Luke knew his Greek poets. And Greek Christians were not unacquainted with contemporary Greek books. Matthew, too, in Jesus' last discourse, in the tremendous picture of the Last Judgment, as we have seen, reflects not a little of the phraseology of the *Testaments of the Twelve Patriarchs,* which he seems to have known in its Greek translation; in particular that of Joseph: 1:5-7

> I was sold into slavery, and the Lord of all
>   made me free:
> I was taken into captivity, and his strong hand
>   succored me.
> I was beset with hunger, and the Lord him-
>   self nourished me.
> I was alone, and God comforted me:
> I was sick, and the Lord visited me:
> I was in prison, and my God showed favour
>   unto me;
> In bonds, and he released me;
> Slandered, and he pleaded my cause;
> Bitterly spoken against by the Egyptians, and
>   he delivered me;
> Envied by my fellow-slaves, and he exalted
>   me.

If we must decline the verdict of antiquity as to
the writer of the Gospel of Matthew, we must seek
another writer for it among the Jewish Christians
of the seventies. He must have been a man familiar
with the utterances of Jesus to such a point that his
representation of them has commanded the attention and adherence of mankind to an amazing degree. It is his Prayer and his Beatitudes and his
Golden Rule, if they are his, that men have accepted
as authentic and satisfying. It is his Sermon on the
Mount, his Parable of the Vineyard, his tremendous
Last Judgment that command our assent if not our
obedience. Luke, too, has his authoritative passages—the Good Samaritan, the Prodigal Son—
which vindicate themselves as authentic, but Luke's
Sermon on the Plain has never overtaken Matthew's
Sermon on the Mount. Its present structure no
doubt owes much to the evangelist, but its materials at all events we find convincingly authentic.

Was there among the apostles a man capable of
such a book, or must we refer it to a contemporary
stranger? The latter seems highly artificial, in the
light of Isaiah's procedure, which resulted in the
Book of Isaiah, a literary fact most undeniable.
There is also Jesus' clear consciousness of Isaiah's
course—its cause and its effect. It was only when
Jesus was threatened with a fate like Isaiah's, Mark
3:6, that he appointed twelve of his followers,
whom he called apostles.

For the Pharisees had left the synagogue and immediately consulted with the Herodians about
Jesus, with a view to putting him to death. Why, the

gospel story has only begun! We have read hardly one-eighth of it, five pages out of forty-two, when the shadow of the Cross falls upon the page. Already Herod's people have marked him for destruction, like John—and as Isaiah had been marked so long before. But Isaiah surmounted it triumphantly, through the writing of his disciples! In fact, the fate of Isaiah has been forgotten, in the presence of his recorded prophecies.

It is clearly a mistake to look for an ordinary man for the role of the author of the Gospel according to Matthew. He was no ordinary man. It was no ordinary man who wrote a Gospel which a French critic, eighteen hundred years later, could call the most important book in the world.

Of course, living for even six months in the companionship of Jesus, hearing him talk and even asking him questions, would be an education of the most intensive kind. And if a man could write and was accustomed to writing, he could hardly help putting some things down. A tax collector was used to doing just that. And then, too, if Jesus had Isaiah's tragic experience and fate in mind (as his choosing the Twelve, after John's enemies turned their attention to him, Mark 3:6, 7, 13, 14, suggests) and Isaiah's great success in making his message survive him, he might well have looked about him for such a man. Isaiah's great words must often have come back to Jesus:

"I will bind up my testimony, and seal my teaching in the heart of my disciples. Then I will wait for the Lord," Isaiah 8:16, 17. Jesus' quotations from

Isaiah in Matthew would fill well-nigh two pages. It was after John's fate was sealed that Jesus chose the Twelve, Mark 3:6, 7, 13, 14. One of them was Matthew, whom he had previously called from his tollhouse to be a disciple, Mark 2:14. And while Jesus is nowhere said to have quoted this saying of Isaiah's, he cannot possibly have missed the measures Isaiah took to enable his message to survive him—and their amazing success! The whole original book of Isaiah, Isaiah 1–39, was, in publication, a posthumous work! I cannot escape the conviction that the choosing of the Twelve was reminiscent of the course taken by Isaiah to perpetuate his message when he was faced with death, and of them all the tax collector seems the only one of Jesus' disciples equipped to seal the testimony, to wait for the Lord's time.

It is obvious that Matthew, with its staggering wealth of Jesus' teaching, overshadowed Mark almost as soon as it appeared, and that is why the collectors of the four Gospels, about A.D. 120, could find only an incomplete copy of Mark to publish in their first edition of the Fourfold Gospel. The most ancient Greek New Testaments, Vaticanus and Sinaiticus, show Mark breaking off abruptly with 16:8—"for they were afraid," and no manuscript or version has ever been found that contained the ending. The familiar conclusion known to us as Mark 16:9–20 has no fitness where it stands and may even belong to some other document—in fact it almost certainly does.

In his *Introduction to the New Testament*, pp. 36,

37, Lake says, "It is generally conceded that the Gospel according to Matthew provides no trace of the genuine ending of Mark. Matthew 28:16–20 seem to be an editorial addition and it is generally held that Matthew, like ourselves, knew Mark only in mutilated form."

On the contrary, a strikingly interesting feature of the relation of Matthew and Mark lies in the concluding narrative of Matthew, the reunion of Jesus with his disciples in Galilee, 28:9, 16–20. This narrative is not found in our Mark, though it is twice predicted, just as though it were about to be narrated; "But after I am raised to life again I will go back to Galilee before you." The idea of reunion in Galilee also reappears in Mark 16:7, almost immediately before the narrative breaks off, when the young man at the tomb tells the women to say to Peter and the disciples,

"He is going before you to Galilee; you will see him there, just as he told you."

Now after Mark breaks off, at 16:8, with the women fleeing frightened from the tomb and telling nobody, because they were afraid, Matthew goes steadily on with the appearance of Jesus to them, repeating the message for the disciples, 28:9, followed in vss. 16–20 with the return of the disciples to Galilee and the Great Commission. It is very clear that this was the conclusion of Mark, which Matthew has faithfully taken over, as his previous use of 14:28 and 16:7 clearly requires, so that we can actually, with a fair degree of certainty, recover the closing twelve lines of Mark from Matthew's faithful use of them in 28:8, 9, 16–20, and thus in a very convincing way bring the earliest Gospel back to its first-century completeness. This may seem an audacious conclusion to reach, but on the basis of what Mark himself forecasts, and what Matthew proceeds to narrate, it brings Mark's narrative to a vigorous and appropriate conclusion.

That Matthew ever composed and circulated a collection of Jesus' sayings in Aramaic seems very unlikely, in view of the general reluctance of people of that time to produce anything resembling a book in Aramaic; no such work has yet been found, unless the Qumran caves provide one. The rabbis were in fact unwilling to have even a *targum* (translation) of parts of the Old Testament written down in Aramaic. And of any book first written in Aramaic we have as yet no knowledge. The short Aramaic life of Darius was a translation of his official life, which was ordered translated into all the languages of his empire, of which Aramaic was one. The short story of Ahiqar has also been found in Aramaic, being apparently a translation from a Mesopotamian (Babylonian?) original, as Clement of Alexandria supposed. Its modern investigators have come to the same conclusion. There was always in the Jewish mind the consciousness that all the books needed for religion had long since been written (the "scripture"), and men had no business trying to improve on it; so says very clearly the Book of Enoch, in the second or first century B.C., "by writing with ink and paper . . . many have sinned from eternity to eternity and until this day.

For men were not created for such a purpose, to give confirmation to their good faith with pen and ink." 69:9, 10. They felt that their Hebrew scriptures contained all the books necessary to religion. Unless the Qumran caves supply them, we have no further hint of an Aramaic literature except some sections of Daniel and Ezra, and a Midrashic piece from Qumran about Sara in Egypt and her physical charms, elaborating Genesis, chapter 12.

Papias' point is that Matthew took down Jesus' sayings in Aramaic and made them available to the Twelve for subsequent consultation. Thus it falls right into line with Isaiah's example, and Jesus' own sudden consciousness of peril.

Nor is it easy for those who so freely deny the authorship of this Gospel by Matthew the apostle to conjure up another figure whom they will admit as its author. They must of course credit him with the most extraordinary understanding of Jesus' message and insight into his teaching. He wrote a book which the keenest literary critics of the western world, eighteen hundred years later, would pronounce the most important book in the world. He was certainly endowed with extraordinary insight into the meaning of Jesus' message, but was not, we are now assured, one of those Jesus selected for that work, or one who was associated with Jesus. Not a personal disciple, they seem to hold; though at every stage of this progress their position seems to become less tenable.

And yet the book was written, improbable as it appears that anyone, known to Jesus or not, could have done it. We seem forced dangerously near the conclusion that it was not written by anybody, yet here it is before all of us, in every Christian home and pulpit.

The question is how a complete stranger to Jesus was able to arrive at the most adequate statement of his teaching that has come down to us, which then received the name of Matthew in defiance of what has been shown to be the unfailing Greek (and Greek Christian) literary practice of the first century. The Greeks did not name books after their barbarian sources, but after the men who wrote them in Greek; that they named the Greek version of the Torah not after Moses, but after its translators into Greek, shows this, as does the naming of the earliest written Gospel not after its apostolic source, the chief of the apostles, but after an obscure assistant named Mark, who had been Peter's interpreter in his last years. The importance Greek Christian readers put upon Greek authorship was of a piece with Greek usage, Jewish (the Septuagint), and pagan, if we understand "Euclid" and all that it had come to mean, and in most of the English-speaking world still means. The probabilities, it appears, are not favorable to this Gospel's having been named after its source instead of its Greek-using author. With this, its authoritative command of Jesus' message startlingly accords. And how better explain this striking fact?

It is not as though there were at hand a rival claimant to the authorship; no scholar has one to suggest, and we are told it was anonymous; it gave no author. But this at once contradicts primitive Christian practice, so strongly under Greek influence, which was averse to anonymity—think of the epigrams! The Greeks had an almost superstitious regard for authorship—even for ten or a dozen lines of it.

But Jesus had already, Mark tells us, selected a disciple—the only individual call anywhere recorded in the Synoptics—Mark 2:14—Levi, the tax collector. Not as an apostle; that plan had not yet matured. It sprang, Mark implies, from the intensifying consciousness of peril. We cannot suppose that Jesus did not remember Isaiah, his favorite prophet, and what his disciples did to preserve and perpetuate his message! Is it possible that Jesus already had hopes for Matthew as his future recorder, if worse came to worst as it had for the prophet Isaiah?

11

the language of the gospel
of matthew

WE cannot escape the feeling that Matthew, or the author of the Gospel that bears his name, has a tendency to be more precise and specific in matters of persons or money than his fellow synoptics. Certainly figures have no terrors for him. After the three fourteens of the genealogy we find the forty days and nights of fasting, followed by three temptations. The word talent, as a sum of money, occurs fourteen times in Matthew but never in Mark, Luke, or John; in fact, nowhere else in the Greek Testament.

In his commentary on Matthew, McNeile pointed out that Matthew uses a hundred and ten words not employed by Mark, Luke or John, or in any other books of the New Testament. Thirty of these words are found in the papyri published in the first three volumes of the Tebtunis papyri, which are predominantly of the second and first centuries before, and the first and second centuries after Christ. My count is a hundred and eleven, perhaps because we were using different Greek text editions. We might fairly expect a somewhat larger vocabulary if our author was a tax collector by profession, and so a professional writer.

About the number of the apostles Matthew is slightly more pointed than his source, Mark, for he repeats the number:

> Then he called his twelve disciples to him, and gave them power over the foul spirits so that they could drive them out, and so that they could heal any disease or illness.
> These are the names of the twelve apostles. . . .
> Jesus sent these twelve out, . . .

Then again in 11:1,

> When Jesus had finished giving his twelve disciples these instructions, . . .

One cannot help noticing that while one mention of their number satisfied Mark and Luke in these conections, Matthew mentions it four times! 10:1, 2, 5, and 11:1, "twelve disciples . . . twelve apostles . . . these twelve . . . twelve disciples." This is suggestive, yet Matthew's Gospel as a whole does not mention the Twelve more often than Luke's, for example. This has the effect of emphasizing them as the recipients of special instruction, of such weight and at such length. Indeed, the instructions given to the Twelve constitute one of the six great discourses of the Gospel of Matthew—a most suggestive fact—and we must wonder how anyone not a member of the Twelve would know them.

We soon see that with the exception of the genealogy there is nothing in Matthew we can stamp as an artificial addiction to numbers for their own sake.

Sometimes he leaves out numbers Mark could supply. Thus, the number of swine in the herd at Gerasa (or Gadara) does not interest Matthew or Luke, though Matthew recorded the number of people fed on two occasions, as given by Mark, only adding to each total, (five thousand, four thousand) "besides women and children," 14:21; 15:38. Our first impression is that this clause so quietly added would in effect multiply the total by two or three, or even more. But we must remember that in Judaism, religion was the concern of the men, and the number of women and children at these gatherings may safely be considered relatively small. Yet the added words stamp Matthew as concerned for general accuracy, if not absolute precision.

The first sentence in the Gospel of Mark transports us to the Book of Isaiah, although to its latter portion, Isaiah 40:3. On his fourth page, Mark is telling us of the call of Levi, or Matthew, the tax collector, Jesus' fifth disciple, who entertains him at his house, an act which evidently impressed Peter. A page further on, the Pharisees and Herodians are uniting to plan Jesus' death; Jesus retreats to the farther side of the Sea of Galilee and meeting the multitude goes up on the mountain and calls to him twelve men, whom he appoints as apostles. The seventh is Matthew. Is this a new course for a prophet? No, for Isaiah, too, had his disciples, and when he was cornered by his enemies, uttered his well-known words, 8:16–18,

"I will bind up my testimony, and seal my teaching in the heart of my disciples. Then I will wait for the Lord, who is hiding his face from the house of Israel; I will set my hope on him."

And shall we not suppose that Jesus, already facing the speedy interruption of his own work by death, as Isaiah's enemy King Manasseh had stopped Isaiah's work, gathered and instructed his disciples, as Isaiah had gathered and instructed his, to defeat the king's measures? The coincidence with Isaiah is more than superficial; it is profound. And are we to suppose Jesus' measures to make sure his teaching survived were any less real and effective than Isaiah's? They were a thousand times more effective, as all the world knows! Jesus did not heroically but dully beat his head against a stone wall; he "sealed his testimony in the heart of his disciples," with a power and skill that have been the marvel of literature and of history. I cannot doubt the heroic action of Isaiah was before his mind, for Isaiah had met a martyr's cruel death, at Manasseh's order, but a few years later the record of his work and his preaching, Isaiah 1–39, preserved till then by the diligence, patience, and courage of his disciples, was offered to the Jewish people, and became in after years the keystone of the great collection of the Prophets. We cannot suppose Jesus was unaware of all this, or indifferent to it. How often he quotes Isaiah and at what length, especially in Matthew—sometimes almost half a page of poetry at a time. And the Book of Isaiah went on to become perhaps the greatest book in the Old Testament—the crowning glory of Hebrew literature, so that oracles men wished to preserve be-

yond the possibility of destruction they added to the
great imperishable Book of Isaiah! They would be
safe there!

The name of the evangelist Matthew, it must be
observed, did little for this Gospel; nobody that
could be named in the whole apostolic circle would
strike the scholarly world—and I speak as a loyal
member of it—as really fit to write the Gospel of
Matthew. Scholars have to take refuge in some
great unknown, whom they make little effort to
describe. But whence the name then?

We are told an Aramaic collection of Jesus' sayings was made by Matthew and became a distinctive source of this Gospel—this on the basis of a remark by Papias of Hierapolis, about A.D. 140. But
we have seen that the Greeks steadily refused to
name books after their (as they considered them)
barbarous sources; why, even the Hebrew Torah,
when it passed into Greek was named after its
seventy Greek-writing translators, the Seventy—
Latin, Septuaginta. The Gospel of Mark, on the
proposed principle, should have been called by the
name of its Aramaic source Cephas, or in Greek,
Peter—but it was not. The whole science of geometry, from whatever sources, was called and is still
generally called by the name of its Greek collector,
translator (and in part, of course, creator)—Euclid!
This attitude is characteristically Greek, and these
books were Greek books. And Matthew was a Greek
book and fell into its place in Greek literature.

Matthew doubtless took down many of Jesus'
sayings in Aramaic; though, in the strongly anti-

literary atmosphere that prevailed among the Jews at that time, that he circulated them as an Aramaic book is hardly probable. We know of no other book composed in Aramaic! The Gospel of Matthew does not sound like it, and leading rabbis objected strongly to the writing down of Aramaic *targums*—translations—even of the Book of Job. But the Greek practice was clearly to name a book for the man who wrote it *in Greek*—never for the barbarous author of its source. The Septuagint is the unfailing and unanswerable obstacle to such a view. Think of it! Naming the books of Moses, not for him, but for the men who translated him into Greek! This is a precedent too little regarded in dealing with the authorship of Matthew. We are reminded that the suggestion of this Aramaic source solution comes from a misunderstanding of Papias of Hierapolis. He was not highly regarded by Eusebius, who says of him, "He appears to have been of very limited understanding, as one can see from his discourses," *Church History* 3:39:13. But Papias' actual statement is, "Matthew took down the sayings in the Hebrew language (meaning Aramaic) and each one translated them as he was able." This remark, embalmed in Eusebius, has caused much confusion, being understood to mean an Aramaic book of Jesus' sayings—a very questionable interpretation.

We see clearly that Greek usage, and especially Greek Christian usage, in the first century named books not after their barbarous sources, but after the men who wrote them in Greek. This was a typically Greek attitude. Other languages simply did not count. It reflects also the Greek sense of authorship; the writer, and particularly the writer in Greek, was what mattered, and all that mattered. We may regret this and even condemn it, but it was certainly the Greek attitude in the first century, and long before. The Christian books of the first century conform to this throughout with the sole exception of Hebrews, which is anonymous, and perhaps intended as a supplement to Paul!

The fact is, there is no real difficulty in accepting Matthew the tax-collector apostle as the author of this great Gospel. It is that authorship that has made him so great that he actually appears too great for his own book! He has literally outdone himself! For think of him for a moment apart from his role as gospel-writer—a despised publican, classed with harlots and outcasts, until Jesus adopted him as a disciple! Why should anyone credit him, a reformed publican, with writing the greatest of first-century Gospels—unless he wrote it? It clearly did nothing for this book to give it Matthew's name, and naming gospels for apostles was not the ancient way of doing, or they would have called the earliest Gospel Peter, not Mark! Who was Mark, anyway? A very secondary, background figure, from the first-century point of view. Consider Acts 15:37–39: Paul and Barnabas are planning the Second Missionary Journey. "Now Barnabas wanted to take John who was called Mark with them. But Paul did not approve of taking with them a man who had deserted them in Pamphylia, instead of going on with them to their work. They differed so sharply about it that they separated, and Barnabas took Mark, and sailed for Cyprus." But Mark later regained Paul's respect (Colossians 4:10), and he was the man who afterward recorded Peter's memories and *put them into Greek,* and that was what mattered. We are again confronted with the Greek regard for authorship—meaning authorship in Greek! This may not be your attitude or mine; doubtless we would have done differently. But this was the Greek attitude, and Christianity had become a Greek movement, which is why it took up the pen and wrote the New Testament.

These two points must be kept in mind: (1) "Authors" were men who wrote in Greek, not barbarous tongues, and (2) A dozen lines were enough to confer literary immortality on one. And yet we find these basic considerations hardly glimpsed by modern writers on the Gospel of Matthew. In such a world how could the writer of the great moving Gospel of Matthew possibly be forgotten?

Is it not fair to say that the Gospel of Matthew presents the fullest and the most trustworthy form of the message and teaching of Jesus? From the Sermon on the Mount to the Parable of the Last Judgment, men steadily resort to it for light on what Jesus thought and desired. We think at once of certain parables of Luke's—the Pharisee and the Publican, the Prodigal Son, the Good Samaritan—but these are the exceptions that prove the rule. Nor is it most probable that the one of Jesus' contemporaries that best stated his ideals and purposes was a man who never saw or heard him or felt the enlightening effect of personal contact with him. Yet this has been generally assumed. This is in part due to the consciousness the writer shows of subsequent events, such as the Jewish War with Rome, a staggering reality when the Gospel was written which no doubt colored its account of Jesus' forecast. Of course the evangelist's mind would inevitably seize and grapple with the things in Jesus' teaching that had come so terribly true.

But when it comes to general matters such as the Lord's Prayer and the Beatitudes, Luke's formulations of these have never rivaled Matthew's. Who uses Luke's Beatitudes, or the curses that accompany them? Everybody uses Matthew's Lord's Prayer and recites his Beatitudes. Nor can we forget that in all the speeches given in the Acts as by Paul, we never detect any of the characteristic Pauline phrases or expressions so familiar to us from his letters, with which Luke was of course totally unacquainted. And yet Paul must have spoken in very much the same terms in which he wrote, or rather, dictated. We can only conclude that Luke is by no means a close reporter. And if for Paul, to some extent, though we believe a less extent, also for Jesus.

Just why the name of Matthew should have been given a book like Matthew, unless he wrote it, has never been shown. Certainly it was given to it and very anciently, well before the middle of the second century—in all probability at least from the publication of the Fourfold Gospel on. The only solution offered is that of Papias—that Matthew had indeed taken down in Aramaic sayings of Jesus which were supposed to have formed the basis of the Gospel of Matthew. But as we have seen, this is precisely the way the Greek reading world did not name Greek books. Their Hebrew or Aramaic writers did not matter; unless they put their books into Greek too! What mattered was who put them into Greek forms which intelligent men, for so the Greeks regarded themselves, could read. In the presence of this commanding fact, so often ignored, Papias' suggestion that an Aramaic taking-down by Matthew of Jesus' sayings lay at the basis of Matthew fades quite away. What if it did? The Greeks took no account of such matters. Their question was, Who put it into Greek? Witness Mark, Luke, Clement, Hermas, John, Euclid, the Septuagint. What is there to be put over against this list? This is a definite question which must be faced and answered by those who so lightly set aside the Matthaean authorship. Probably Matthew did both things: took down Jesus' sayings in Aramaic and later published them in Greek.

It is a far easier thing to expand a book already written than to conceive and create one wholly *de novo*. Matthew, long accustomed to the early expectation of the end of the world and the return of Jesus to the earth, would see no room or need for writing books about him. But the sudden martyrdom of Peter and the consequent appearance of Mark and the welcome it received—for it was not allowed to perish, but was widely and warmly welcomed by Greek Christians—showed at once the

place in Christian life waiting for such works. And
the writer of Matthew, whoever he was, had the
material for a larger, better book for the Greek
Christian public. The evident usefulness of Mark
showed him the need for such Christian books, and
what value they might have to the Christian cause.
He could not withhold what he had to contribute
to it.

And this solution strikingly accords with touches
already mentioned; Isaiah quoted by name seven
times for a total of a page or more; his strange
saying, 8:16, 17; "I will bind up my testimony, and
seal my teaching in the heart of my disciples. Then
I will wait for the Lord, who is hiding his face from
the house of Israel," is not quoted in Matthew, but
comes to our minds as we read how Jesus, hearing
of John's arrest, retreated to Galilee, 4:12, and began to gather disciples about him, 4:18–20. He
preached the Sermon on the Mount, 5:1–7:27, and
soon after called another disciple, named Matthew,
as he sat at the tollhouse, 9:9, the first addition that
he records to the original quartette of fishermen,
Simon Peter, Andrew, James and John. But the
Twelve were being gathered, for in 10:1, he called
his twelve disciples unto him, and eighth among
them "Matthew the tax-collector." Mark too accepts
this name for him, although in 2:14 he calls him
Levi. Luke, too, calls him Levi, 5:27, 28, and places
the dinner that followed his call in Levi's house.
Yet on the very next page Luke calls the seventh
apostle Matthew, 6:14. As Matthew and Luke
clearly had Mark's Gospel before them, they are

evidently changing Levi to Matthew; only Matthew's Gospel does not call him Levi at all, even at his call, but Matthew.

Mark describes Jesus' removal to Galilee and the beginning of his preaching of the good news of the reign of God, 1:14, 15, as triggered by the arrest of John the Baptist. Mark also connects the call of the Twelve with the plotting of the Herodians and Pharisees to kill Jesus, 3:6. One is reminded of Isaiah's disciples, on whom he so relied to carry on his message, whatever befell him. We cannot doubt that Jesus had Isaiah's course and his fate before his mind, in choosing and training the Twelve. In Matthew's Gospel his quotations from Isaiah are especially long and frequent; printed as poetry, as we have seen and as they should be, they would make over a page of Matthew.

We must constantly remember that somebody, in the first century, wrote the Gospel of Matthew. Is it any easier to postulate some unknown person, who had never heard or known Jesus, finding the Gospel of Mark, using the whole of its contents, transposing its materials to suit himself, finding one or two other minor sources and putting in their materials, but above all setting forth Jesus' teaching with such extraordinary immediacy that most scholars think it a genuine representation of what he taught? Nobody could have made it up, except somebody at least as great as he!

For someone certainly wrote the Gospel of Matthew; it exists. We must earnestly consider the probability of a stranger to Jesus, or perhaps one who

had casually seen or heard him, coming across the
Gospel of Mark, feeling the vigor of its action, but
distressed at its confused introduction, and the de-
ficiency of its account of Jesus' teaching, aware also
of one or two other short accounts of Jesus' teaching,
setting himself to put all these together into one
Gospel, which should embody the values of all of
them. Something compels this supposed author, unknown by name to history or literature, to make
these narratives the vehicle for the most exalted and
gripping account of Jesus' teaching ever written.

The tradition, however, is that one of Jesus' apostles, by profession the most literate of them, perhaps
like Isaiah's disciples, specially commissioned by
him to record and preserve his message, kept in
memory or writing what he thought its greatest
features, not writing them out into a book, for the
time was to be short! Then the Gospel of Mark
appears. But how faulty! No adequate introduction!
Not in the historical order as the new writer remembers it, and so weak in Jesus' teaching! Then
as so often happens, one book suggested the better
book that could be written. But how does the writer
know that Mark's order was at fault? How indeed,
unless he was himself an active participant; he was
there and himself witnessed the action, as Mark did
not. It must be remembered that Peter never saw
Mark's gospel, to pass upon the accuracy of its order.

Are we ready to suppose that a later convert, such
as Luke was, who had never heard Jesus, had this
loftier vision of his message, this clearer idea of the
sequence of the gospel action and of the order of

the teaching documents that had come into his hands? That possibility must be patiently weighed, of course, but does not prove either stimulating or fruitful.

The Greek public for which Matthew was written was thoroughly accustomed to works that frankly named their authors. The great Oxford lexicon of 1940, Liddell-Scott-Jones, devotes twenty-three pages to listing Greek authors, whose number reaches the amazing total of twelve hundred. All in all, the Greek authors listed, including the chief Epigrammatists, prior to A.D. 100, will make a total of six hundred and twenty, without early Christian writers or most Jewish writers in Greek. And in the *Anthology*, as we have seen, even writers of a single epigram, no matter how short, were faithfully included—Ammianus, Eutroclus, Pinytus!

But consider in the Hebrew lexicon what authors can be named. It gives us no list, but perhaps fifteen can be tentatively listed in the Old Testament period! Does not this simple statistic tell the story? Fifteen versus six hundred and twenty gives us the background of our problem of authorship with terrific force. It is another world.

The Greek had no mind for anonymity. He expected to know whose book he was reading. That went without saying. It was understood. It was a situation well known to Greek readers and to Greek writers. With Mark, the Christian movement enters that world and meets its conditions. If Matthew is to write in Greek he cannot escape this demand.

12

the gospel of antioch

LET us seek to gather up some of the considerations we have dealt with and the conclusions we have reached. We have noted that Christian literature began among Greek converts, in an age that was reasonably active in writing and publishing Greek books. We remind ourselves that the publication of books in Greek or Latin was freely practiced in the first century; slave labor made the multiplication of elegant copies easy. A "reader" with a room full of such slaves, often better educated than their Roman masters, could easily produce a substantial edition of a small book in a month or so, and the handwriting in some of the Latin copies was so good that modern English type designers take them as their models. Martial, a contemporary of Luke, was charged by his critics with publishing only a book a year! Publishing must not be confused with printing, or the medieval situation in book-making with the situation, Greek and Latin, in the first century. Martial, vulgar fellow though he was, could name four bookstores in Rome where his books, "smoothed with pumice and smart with purple," could be bought. A private house in Pompeii destroyed by Vesuvius in the famous eruption of A.D. 79, contained a library of eight hundred scrolls, mostly charred by the heat of course, but suggestive of what libraries the houses of cultivated people contained, in the very days when the New Testament was being written—and published. Cicero had a library in each of his numerous villas.

And publication made a great difference. Mark, Matthew, Luke, Acts show no literary influence of Paul, in A.D. 70, 80, 90—then Paul's letters are published, probably at Ephesus, and from then until now it would be hard to find a Christian writing uninfluenced by Paul's letters! Such was the difference publication made. This was the world for which the Gospels were written. And how that world responded to them! In twenty-five years they were not three but four, and published together—The Gospel —according to Matthew, according to Mark, according to Luke, according to John, and that collection has led the world in publication ever since. For what book rivals it in sheer circulation today? Mark and Matthew were the first books ever published in the language of the plain people.

My point is, they were not obscure or esoteric. They were in the forefront of the reading world's attention. And Matthew's name literally led all the rest. There is nothing obscure about it. His is the most conspicuous name in Christian literature and of course one of the most important. It cannot be explained as an oversight. His book is surpassed in the New Testament, in length, but not in influence,

only by Luke's two volumes, each of which is a page
or two longer.

Matthew, the most conspicuous name in Christian
literature, is the name that we are asked by many
scholars to dismiss as a mistake, a blunder, or a de-
ception. It is evident that this is most improbable.
To begin with, it is too conspicuous. And very
powerful evidence certainly must be brought to support this claim. There must be a sharp and glaring
inconsistency between the authorship of this Gospel
and what we can learn of Matthew, the tax collector
of Capernaum.

We have seen that there is no such inconsistency,
but that on the contrary, it would have been utterly
unlike Greek habits of the day to have let the
writer's name perish from human memory. Too
many discussions of the question have proceeded in
entire obliviousness of Greek regard for authorship
and determination to let nothing obscure it. But as
we have seen, the Greeks of the first century cared
nothing about what barbarian sources a writer
might have employed. And the more we learn about
the tax collectors of the Greek world in the first
century, the likelier does the tax-collector author of
the leading Gospel appear.

It is agreed that the Gospel of Matthew arose in
Antioch. It was then the third city in the Roman
world. Rome was of course the first, and it was there
that the earliest Gospel was written. Alexandria was
the second city in the empire, but official dread of
anti-Jewish riots delayed the Christian mission to it
for some time. But Antioch, the third city in the

empire, the wickedest of them all, we are told, was the scene of the first Greek mission, so ably prosecuted by Barnabas and his young protégé Saul of Tarsus. The Jewish war of A.D. 66–70 drove many Christians and Jews of Judea and Galilee to take refuge in Antioch; that exodus is reflected in Matthew 24:15–22; "Those who are in Judea must fly to the hills." The Christian mission in Antioch so firmly established by Barnabas and Saul was further reinforced and its missionaries were sent far and wide. Antioch became the basic city of the Greek mission—a most appropriate place for the appearance of the greatest of the Gospels.

But how strangely improbable that Christianity's finest literary expression should appear on such a world stage cloaked in anonymity! Does not such an origin strike us as most unlikely? Surely Antioch knew who wrote this great book, and its authorship could hardly be concealed. It may very well be that the Antioch leaders encouraged Matthew to do this; Mark had no doubt been written, ten years before, under strong encouragement from the Greek Christians of Rome. But Matthew was no name to conjure with; it was this Gospel that made him famous in Christian literary annals. His name before A.D. 75 or 80 was little known or regarded. Mark tells of his call as a disciple, and the dinner he gave for Jesus, Mark 2:14, 15. Zaccheus did as much a few months later, in Jericho, Luke 19:2–9. But Matthew was afterward included in the twelve apostles, though he remains very much of a lay figure in all the Gospels thereafter. Yet his profession with its necessary proficiency in books and records makes a not inappropriate background for just such a task. For one thing, if he were not the author, why would the Christians of Antioch call it by the name of a man of so unsavory a calling? And in many respects the Gospel of Matthew fairly reflects a tax collector's background. Antioch can hardly have been unaware of the identity of the author of a new Gospel of such extraordinary appeal and authority. The old apostle must have been teaching it to them for years.

None of the Gospels we observe was written in Judea or Galilee or even in what we think of as the Holy Land. Christian literature was definitely of metropolitan origin; in fact its next great creative center was to be Ephesus! It was a religion not of the deserts or the solitudes but of the busiest and most crowded metropolises of the Roman world, a faith not of hermits and anchorites but of the *agora* and the lecture hall—a definitely urban religion.

As we seek to recover and reconstruct the attitudes and measures of the first publishers of what we know as the Gospel according to Matthew, we observe that there was already one written Gospel in circulation—the Gospel of Mark, which was presumably known simply as "the Gospel," or "the Gospel of Jesus Christ," Mark 1:1, where the name of the book that follows is plainly given; the title is not to be understood as part of the first sentence, as it was by Tyndale, Coverdale and their successors down to and including the King James version, from 1611 until today. This was corrected in the Revised Version of 1881 and most modern translations.

The publication of the second Gospel, known to us as Matthew, immediately created a problem: How were they to be distinguished? Matthew had to have a distinctive name from the time of its appearance, or very soon after. From its wealth of Jesus' teaching, it evidently accepted the designation of a "gospel." The preposition *kata*, "according to," may well have been introduced when the Fourfold Gospel collection was formed and published, about A.D. 120; it has in part a distributive feeling— the part by Matthew, the part by Mark, etc.—the whole composing the Gospel. But in their first years the Gospel of Mark and the Gospel of Matthew may have been used. Mark indeed is quite specific; "The beginning of" (that is, Here begins) "the Gospel of Jesus Christ," and this, or "The Gospel," was evidently its original name; the later "Memoirs of Peter" is not found in pre-Catholic Christian literature, or prior to Irenaeus.

We have seen that the Greek way of naming books and writers was to give Greek versions of such earlier records of Oriental origin the names of their Greek translators, since they felt that it was only when they passed into Greek that they became intelligible and thus real to the Greek world they so highly prized. If Matthew was merely based upon a work by Matthew, it would not bear his name. Look at Mark; it rested back on Peter's preaching. Why, then, is it not called the Gospel of Peter? Because Peter did not write it, and write it in Greek. That was what to the Greek mind made it literature, and introduced it to the intelligent world. If Matthew had written some underlying document of it and left it there, they would not have given it his name. It must bear the name of the man who put it forth in Greek, for the edification and enjoyment of men who read Greek. This is a point of literary-historical probability that is easily supported, as we have seen. For, as Mark did not enter the Greek world as "Peter," though it owed so much to him, (and as the Greek version of the Torah had lost the name of Moses, its traditional author, and received the generalized name of its supposed translators, "The Seventy,") Matthew could not have achieved that name on the ground that it went back in part at least to an Aramaic proto-Matthew, subsequently put into Greek by a later hand. The Greek mind would at once demand, "Whose hand?" and inevitably give it that translator's name. Yet modern learning has almost unanimously disregarded this general Greek practice in nomenclature and assumed that if Matthew rests on a basic Semitic document, such as the supposed logia, that would adequately explain its ascription to Matthew. Not at all; unless he also himself composed the whole work and put it into Greek. In fact, the supposed inclusion of a Matthean Sayings document in our Matthew is hardly more than incidental to its bearing Matthew's name. It is ascribed to Matthew as its Greek author, from no matter what sources or basic document. That is the way the Greeks looked at books.

There is above all the improbability that in the Greek atmosphere in which the Gospels arose the

name of the author of the leading Gospel should
have been overlooked and forgotten, particularly if
there was already one book of the same type in circulation. We know the names of the other early
evangelists—Mark, Luke, John—and why not Matthew? Manuscript tradition is in no uncertainty
about it, as far back as it goes. It must be remembered that in the Greek Gospels we are not in a
Jewish atmosphere, which usually did not recognize
personal authorship. We remember Eduard Meyer
and his remark that Oriental literature was anonymous; the Hebrew prophets rising like islands out of
a sea of anonymity! That is not true of the Gospels
for a moment!

The question naturally occurs to us, Has the
Gospel of Matthew ever been ascribed to anyone
else? Or has a nameless figure more likely than Matthew to have written it ever been described or de-
vised? We cannot learn that one has. And yet the
Gospel of Matthew is a fact of literature, not to be
denied, which stood up in antiquity so command-
ingly that it became the leading book in the Fourfold Gospel and the whole New Testament.

The picture is of a disciple of Jesus, chiefly
concerned with his teaching and ministry, telling
his stories for half a century and then upon
the arrival of the new Gospel of Mark in
Antioch, rewriting them with its aid. There is
nothing improbable about this. The expectation of Jesus' early return on the clouds of heaven
would deter the apostle from writing a book
about his earthly ministry for months and then

for years. When was his promised coming? It continued to be vaguely expected, as some earnest people expect it still! The arrival of the Gospel of Mark in Antioch, about A.D. 70 or soon after, creates a situation which leads Matthew to record his memories and perhaps his memoranda of Jesus and his teaching. Mark's confused beginning, which still perplexes even his commentators, especially 1:13, with its obscure allusion to Psalm 91:11–13, must be remedied, and Matthew offers an introduction that is positively commanding, 1:1–4:17. For one thing, it is one-eighth as long as the whole Gospel of Mark.

Moreover, we are dealing with Greek writing which had little use for anonymity. Think of the epigrams of the early centuries and the volumes of the *Anthology* that they compose! One great epigram of only half a dozen lines would bring literary immortality.

Picture the situation. The Christian body in Antioch, a great Greek church, deeply concerned with the mission to the Greek world, with its Christian outposts in Ephesus, Philippi, Corinth, and Rome, awakes to the Gospel of Mark; the first Christian book to make its appearance; the moving story of the great Christian tragedy. It is a startling and stirring experience for this leading Christian group, especially as coming not from themselves, but from what must seem an outpost in the Christian warfare —faraway Rome—so lately just one of their mission stations. Think of it! A Christian book! Is Christianity then to enter the field of books and writing?

The success of Mark's little book gives the answer; the Greek world loved books, and welcomed them, and the Gospel's future was in the Greek world! And to someone at Antioch possessed of the materials of Jesus' teaching comes the idea of the better book that may be written. Did he write it secretly? Or were the Antioch leaders in some sort of touch with his enterprise? Certainly, there was no secret about its authorship in such a city as Antioch, when it appeared. We cannot doubt that Antioch was back of it, as Christian Rome was back of the Gospel of Mark.

In the seventies Jerusalem was in ruins. Antioch was the center of Christianity; we may almost say its birthplace! It was there that Christianity received its name, Acts 11:26; "The disciples first came to be known as Christians, at Antioch." Antioch was, in Harnack's fine phrase, the first fulcrum of Christianity. Ephesus would have its day in the nineties and after—and what a day! But it was in Antioch that the Gospel of Matthew made its appearance—not in some rural setting, remote and obscure, but where Christianity was at its height and peak—the third city of the empire, the birthplace of the Greek mission. Christianity came to itself in Antioch. Its missionaries went forth to evangelize Asia Minor, and then to carry the gospel into Europe, the continent of its destiny!

On such a stage and in such a time, how could its author escape identification? The Christians of Antioch were Greeks, and the Greeks admired authorship; they revered and remembered it. They

required and demanded it! In such a place and at
such a time, the writer of this great Gospel could
hardly fail of identification. Particularly when it had
to compete with an earlier Gospel, whose author's
name was known, anonymity would be out of the
question. Any Greek, hearing of it, would instinctively say,

"Another Gospel? Who wrote it?"

conclusion

THERE are eight considerations that may guide us to a sounder conclusion as to the authorship of the Gospel of Matthew:

1. The Isaiah background and the course the prophet took so effectively in a similar situation.

2. The call of Matthew—detached, and unexplained.

3. The Greek regard for authors; they demanded authorship even for a poem two lines long.

4. The tax collector touches.

5. The Antioch origin—the stage of such important Christian beginnings; the Greek mission, first local, then empire-wide; source of the distinctive name of the Greek believers, and the like.

6. Matthew's subsequence to Mark and use of practically all of that first written Gospel.

7. The testimony of Papias.

8. The unbroken Christian tradition that Matthew wrote it.

With the earliest Gospels written in Greek and published, Christianity had become a Greek movement. This happened at Antioch, where Christianity received its name, never since changed, and set about its world-wide mission. Jewish habits of anonymity were gone. And—most conclusive—Matthew is not even the earliest Gospel! That was Mark, doubtless already so known, since Mark was the indispensable link with Peter. This multiplies the difficulty of supposing Matthew anonymous, tenfold! Mark might possibly circulate as the Gospel, as long as it was the only one; but when Matthew made its appearance, Matthew simply had to have a name of its own, did it not? Among the Greek Christians of Antioch, "Who wrote it?" would be the inevitable question—unless they had already recognized the familiar language of their old friend Matthew, the tax collector who became an apostle!

index

160

DATE DUE